The Homecraft Book

ANN HATHAWAY

Copyright © 2015 Pillar International Publishing Ltd

All rights reserved.

Cover Image: Zoodle Design

Book design: Lotte Bender

ISBN-13: 978-1515356028

DEDICATION

Dedicated to Cepta, Ann and Gerry – the survivors

ANN HATHAWAY

ACKNOWLEDGMENTS

Without the help of Liz Coffey, Pauline O'Dwyer, Emmet Jackson and Lotte Bender this project would have been greatly diminished. Deepest thanks.

Contents

Introduction — *page 3*

Foreword — *page 9*

The Daily Round — *page 11*

Work of the House — *page 19*

Household Hints — *page 37*

Substitutes — *page 42*

Uses for old Articles — *page 44*

Waste not, Want not! — *page 49*

Good Ideas — *page 53*

Economy Hints — *page 58*

Stains — *page 60*

Getting rid of Pests — *page 67*

Seasonable Hints — *page 69*

Washing and Ironing — *page 75*

The Needlewoman — *page 85*

Beauty — *page 93*

Health — *page 111*

Dress — *page 118*

Recipes — *page 124*

Cookery Hints — *page 136*

Introduction

By

Thaddeus Lovecraft, grandson of Ann Hathaway

1. Preamble

The advice contained in this book is to be followed at the reader's own risk. The publisher, deceased author and grandchild admit no liability if, through absence of common-sense or absence of health and safety training, the reader(s) injures/burns/shames/eviscerates herself/himself/themselves or another party or parties.

2. Post-War Women's Issues

In today's consumerist world we are inundated by adverts for products and services which will help make women's lives healthier, cleaner, fitter, trimmer, flatter, browner, more regular, less itchy, better smelling and less blotchy. As an anodyne escape from the pressure of keeping-up, we imagine life was easier long ago. We think of our mothers and grandmothers and how much simpler and wholesome their lives were. But were they?

Ann Hathaway, post-war goddess of all things feminine, has left us a fabulous historical document in her publication 'The Homecraft Book', first published in 1945 to universal acclaim. Therein, amongst other nuggets of household wisdom, she lists the health and beauty problems of the day and their remedies. Let me catalogue but a few, so that you may be disabused of any naïve notions about 'The good old days'.

A brief scan of the text shows that the beauty issues of the day included: dry skin, undernourished skin, greasy skin, enlarged pores, blackheads, spotty complexion, tired skin, lines, freckles, wrinkles, coarse skin, cold sores, tired eyes, eye strain, underdeveloped eyelashes, red nose, stained teeth, heavy or sagging jaw, hollow cheeks, dull hair, yellowing hair, dandruff, smoker's hair, greasy hair, prematurely grey hair, congestion of the scalp, feeble head circulation, dark shoulders, pimply arms, plump arms, sandpaper elbows, stained hands, enlarged knuckles, large legs, thick ankles, obstinate sandpaper knees, soft corns, heel lumps, thick waist, blotchiness, too pale, not pale enough, discoloured neck, muddy complexion and obesity.

Right now, your innate suggestibility, the manna of the marketing guru, is saying - 'Are they talking about me?' - as you ponder your engorged knuckles whilst scratching your congested scalp. Do you have obstinate sandpaper knees? Are your shoulders off the pale scale? I think we both know you do and they are.

Fear not, because Ann Hathaway does not come with problems alone, she also comes with solutions. Of course, you will have to buy the book to find out how to resolve your post-war beauty problems.

3. Essentials for the Post-War Shopping Basket

In *'The Homecraft Book'* Ann Hathaway details solutions to a thousand and one domestic dilemmas. For your delectation, amusement and enrichment, I will list some of the key items that you will need to purchase, if you are to lead the organised, economical and aesthetically superior life of the post-war housewife.

1. Cruets and castors.
   Over time we have become accustomed to using the manufacturer's vessels for oil, vinegar, salt, pepper and mustard. That must stop immediately. We must also purchase a mustard spoon.
2. Borax.
   This we use to stop kettles furring. Alas, it can no longer be purchased over the counter as ingestion may cause gastrointestinal distress including nausea, persistent vomiting, abdominal pain, and diarrhoea. A modern solution to furring is to throw the kettle out and buy another one.
3. Quicklime.
   We use this to repair cracks in china cups, plates and saucers. According to Wikipedia – "Quicklime causes severe irritation when inhaled or placed in contact with moist skin or eyes. Inhalation may

cause coughing, sneezing, laboured breathing. It may then evolve into burns with perforation of the nasal septum, abdominal pain, nausea and vomiting."

4. Ammonia.

Banish shabby umbrellas by rubbing them with ammonia and warm water. Ammonia will not kill you but it will dispatch your aquatic pets to the great aquarium in the sky. The modern taste for goldfish and terrapins has doubtless led to the trend of discarding shabby umbrellas in park bins and on busy roads.

5. Peroxide of Hydrogen.

What a multi-purpose wonder this is! We use Peroxide of Hydrogen to remove yellowing from our bone knife handles. I'm not sure where the hyphen goes in 'bone knife handles'. Wherever I place it, the result is quite macabre. Either the knife is for cutting bones or the knife handle is made of bones. Maybe the knife is used to make bone knife handles? I'm going to leave the hyphen out for now.

When we're not whittling bones to make knife handles, we are conscious of our appearance – that's why we use Peroxide of Hydrogen to burn off our freckles.

6. Eau de Cologne.

You might imagine that we use this to cover up the odour caused by all the vomiting, diarrhoea and dead terrapins but you'd be wrong. We use this to clean our diamond rings and our packs of playing cards.

7. Gin.

    However tempted you may be - don't drink it! You're going to need it to make an astringent for your greasy skin.

8. Boric Crystals.

    We use this to make our eyes sparkle. Boric acid has not yet proven to be carcinogenic but tests in dogs have shown that it can cause testicular atrophy. Women only, then.

9. Lemon Juice.

    Even though the house is positively awash with Peroxide of Hydrogen, we will use lemon juice to bleach the yellow out of our grey hair, giving us the perfect head of silver, lemony hair.

10. Colourless Iodine.

    We use this to treat your enlarged knuckles. This will also fight fungal infection in toenails. If you have any left over after daubing your hideous knuckles and revolting feet, drink it as an expectorant to help move that stubborn phlegm. You disgust me.

11. Cascara Sagrada and Impecacuanha.

    As if life doesn't offer up enough opportunities for purging, your medicine cupboard would be bereft without these exotic-sounding laxatives and emetics.

12. Mustard.

    We rub mustard on the hands to remove the smell of onions. What we use to remove the smell of mustard is not documented. Mustard spoon required.

ANN HATHAWAY

There! Your trip to the cornershop will be filled with wonder and excitement as you embark on your post-war housewife experience. Now, please enjoy this book safely and in a controlled manner.

FOREWORD

In the course of her everyday work the young housewife has to face and overcome a great variety of domestic duties and difficulties. Even the most experienced will frequently come up against problems which they find by no means easy to solve. Every little contribution to the clearing up of doubts about "how to do it" must be welcome to the busy housewife. When her own experience is not up to telling her what is best to be done, it is a boon to be told what somebody else has found effective in similar circumstances. Even when we think we know, it should not be forgotten that newer and better ways of doing dozens of little jobs are being constantly discovered. A change of method will often mean a saving of time, energy or material.

In my long experience as Domestic Correspondent I have been the recipient of a host of enquiries about every imaginable domestic matter—cradles and cookery, needlework and gardening, health and beauty, making, mending, cleaning and preserving, and a dozen-and-one other subjects of interest to every woman. I have also received a continuous stream of information embracing every aspect of homecraft.

With a vast store of valuable material on hands, and an evident need for it in some handy reference form, I felt it a duty to make as much as possible of it available to the many seeming to require it. I have compiled THE HOMECRAFT BOOK *with that object in view. It contains a really great variety of picked hints, ranging over every activity in the home. The sections have been made to cover as wide a field as was possible in a volume which could be published at a price within everybody's reach. With the material still on hands I hope to produce several similar volumes to complete a comprehensive domestic reference library. I will welcome suggestions for incorporation in further issues.*

For much of the material on which I have worked I am indebted to practical housewives all over the country. I take this opportunity of expressing my appreciation of their interest in my Domestic Corner, and my gratitude for their valuable contributions, many of which I have taken the liberty of including in this book.

It is my sincere hope that every purchaser will enjoy reading THE

ANN HATHAWAY

HOMECRAFT BOOK *as much as I have enjoyed compiling it. Also that it will prove as useful and helpful as my own experience leads me to believe it will.*

Ann Hathaway.

The Daily Round

WORK TO PLAN:

Every housewife should organise her work as a man organises his business. Homes, like business undertakings, differ in dozens of ways. There are old and new houses, small and large families, and variations in equipment and resources. Obviously the same rules and methods cannot be generally applied. There are, nevertheless, certain basic principles which may be taken as a guide in the administration and organisation of every home, big or small; these principles are best made apparent by a critical examination of the daily round common to all housewives. Even in the many cases where a combination of circumstances make the housewife's lot well-nigh impossible, because of having too much to do and being forced to do it without help, applied efficiency may do much to ease the strain. In the paragraphs which follow, we will discuss how duties in the daily round may be organised, and where improved methods may be possible.

ESSENTIALS FIRST:

The housewife divides her time between three classes of work. These three may be described as (1) Essential—work which must be done every day; (2) Extras—work requiring regular, but not necessarily daily, attention; and

(3) Hobbies—various odds and ends of work done by choice. The first is obviously the one to be considered in any planned day. A very little thought will quickly marshal in their regular order, those duties which must be carried through every day of the year. Preparation and serving of meals and washing up; airing and tidying of bedrooms; making beds, general sweeping, dusting and tidying of rooms in constant use; attention to fireplaces in season and, finally, shopping (foodstuffs). The meals routine will be regulated by the working hours of the members of the household and various other circumstances to which special later reference will be necessary; but it should be the efficient housewife's practice to tackle and finish all essential work before considering any work in either of the other two classes.

AN AVERAGE HOME:

We must strike a likely average, so let's take a house of five or six rooms (excluding kitchen and bathroom) and a family of four or five. Adjustments will be necessary according to whether it is a family of all adults, or including children. There is no maid-servant. There is no Hoover. As already agreed, meals are excluded from the consideration of essential duties for the moment, so we will suppose it is nearly 9.0 a.m., and breakfast is just one.

MORNING WORK:

Here, then, is our morning's work. Turn back beds, open up windows to air bedrooms, collect odds and ends for wash-basket. Back to kitchen, wash up breakfast things and leave kitchen tidy. Clear, clean and re-set firegrates in use. Dust hall door, rub letter-box, sweep porch and step. Sweep and tidy dining-room and sittingroom. Make beds, tidy bedrooms, clean up bathroom, sweep stairs and hall, and finish downstairs dusting; and we find it is already gone 11.0 a.m.!

Too much for two hours and a half? Well we'll see!

ESTABLISH THE CONDITIONS:

A half-neglected house is not going to be spick and span after a couple of hours' hurried attention. There must first be certain conditions established before we can hope to regularly complete our essential housework by 11.0 a.m.—or thereabouts. If things have fallen badly behind we must give ourselves a fresh start by getting help from somebody to straighten up and clean the place from top to bottom. Once thoroughly waxed and polished all your linoleum and surrounds will look good for weeks, with a light sweeping and quick rub with a slightly oily mop—a few minutes' work in each room if done every day. Overcrowding with furnishings, ornaments, etc., means waste of time and labour. You can make rooms comfortably cosy without "cluttering." Get rid of surplus articles—they only make work for you. Every article you have to lift for dusting means so much time cut from your scanty (if any) leisure.

FAMILY CO-OPERATION:

If the housewife is to have a fair chance, the whole family must co-operate. Thoughtless, lazy or untidy members should be made sit up. Adults should at least be able to look after their own clothes and belongings. Any child over four years of age can be quickly trained to do the same. Garments strewn around bedrooms—shaving tackle lying around the hand-basin—books thrown anywhere but on the shelf. These things (and many other similar) should not be tolerated. Offenders should be made to realise how very unfair it is to impose on the average housewife's willingness to accept the dozen-and-one "valeting" jobs which no considerate person would consider part of her routine work. It's something worth having a row about!

SPLIT THE DIFFERENCE:

Let the rule of the house be: "A place for everything

and everything in its place." Intelligently applied, it will hurt nobody and benefit all. Extremes should be avoided; the members of the household cannot be expected to carry a duster about with them. Reasonable latitude must be allowed. Assuming then that her home is in good condition to start with, and she has the co-operation of the family in maintaining tidiness, the average housewife should manage to get through the essential morning programme, already suggested, in about two hours and a half. This programme can be adjusted to suit individual circumstances; stairs or upstairs passages may only need attention every second day if traffic is fairly limited. Twice a week may suffice to give more than cursory care to a little used sittingroom. Experiment will show how available morning time may be apportioned between the several demands on it.

ADVANCE SHOPPING LIST:

Morning work concluded, attention to the mid-day meal—luncheon or dinner—is our next concern. What is the menu to be? The efficient housewife knows; she has selected to-day's bill of fare yesterday evening. It is the only really satisfactory way of ensuring a pleasing variation of meals and their trouble-free preparation. In the evening, when you have time to relax a little, plan the menu of the following. Use your pencil and paper to prepare a shopping list, and do not forget to provide alternative items in cases where prices may vary to an extent likely to carry you beyond the amount you have budgeted. Then, the following day you know exactly what you have to buy, the time you will need for cooking and preparing the selected foodstuffs, and you can go about the work without any bother, confusion or uncertainty.

SHOPPING FOR FOODSTUFFS:

Shop personally; you can then select exactly what you want and also make sure of the price and weight being correct. Most shops will deliver the goods if you don't want to take them home yourself. Give yourself ample time to make your purchases. Find out which shop serves your purpose best with regards to prices and quality—preferably a local shop; but a shopping trip to town, once or twice a week, may often save you many times your bus fare. Don't buy things you really don't want just because they're cheap, doing so usually results in waste except with tinned goods or foods that can be stored, when it is advisable to take advantage of any cheap lots you see for sale.

DISCOURAGE RUNNING BUFFETS:

It will make quite a difference in the daily round if the mid-day meal hour can be arranged to have all members of the family sit to table together. Varying luncheon intervals at places of business sometimes cause the meal to be spread over two or three hours. This inconvenience may be overcome by taking the principal meal in the evening, or only one person may be quite unsuited to the fixed hour and may be agreeable to have a moderately substantial dinner during the day, making up with a light tea-time snack at home. Trying to keep meals hot and delaying after-dinner washing-up are snags worth trying to eliminate. Such inconveniences are often accepted from force of habit. A little planning may easily overcome them.

SPECIAL DUTIES:

Her essential work completed, the housewife must consider what may be termed special duties. These are mainly: washing, collecting and sending soiled linen, etc., to laundry; cleaning windows (inside), cleaning silver, aluminium, cutlery, etc.; special turning out of rooms in succession; ironing; baking; special polishing (hall and stairs); carpet-cleaning; washing paintwork. The best time for such work is the interval between the mid-day meal and tea-time. A fixed afternoon each week for one or other task may be found most practical or the work may be taken at convenient times regulated according to governing circumstances. The main thing is to spread attention to special duties over the whole six days.

ABOUT THE BABIES:
When there is a baby in the home—or two or three young children—all rules and regulations must be considered subject to the attentions necessarily devoted to their special needs. The regular feeding of a baby—the occasional illnesses that come to every youngster—extra washing and mending—all will inevitably cut across the planned daily routine. Mother must accommodate herself to circumstances. She will very likely have to skimp things temporarily in other directions. Some things which she would ordinarily like to do every day must be tackled only every second day, and so on. Half the battle is won if the planned routine is adhered to strictly with the children as with every other activity. Fixed times for feeding, bathing, sleeping, and their every regular daily need, will be best for the children themselves and will facilitate the readier gauging and rationing of time for other duties. It will make a very great difference if the harassed housewife can afford to get in an outside help once a fortnight or thereabouts to scrub down the house and keep the very heavy parts of her housework from falling too far behind.

REST ASSURED:
The programme already suggested in these little pars., packing the greater part of the housewife's duties into the morning and early afternoon—will be difficult to manage in many cases. It is a fact, nevertheless, that going all out to achieve results early in the day will be well rewarded by the evening's rest and freedom. Even when some jobs overflow, and have got to be taken out of their time, they may be handled in a more leisurely way than when done under the duress imposed by the lack of a methodical

routine. Keep the prospect of the care-free evening in mind when the work of the day tends to pall. It will make things easier.

The whole objective of our planning and plotting is to try to ensure that some little part of the day may be claimed as her own by the efficient housewife. To be able to sit down for a couple of hours every evening with a book to read, or to indulge in any other restful pastime, is a necessity; to be able to do so in the knowledge that no duty has been neglected is a comfort and a joy. Then may the cares and the worries of the day be put aside and the luxury of complete relaxation enjoyed to the full. In the presence of friends' company, the desultory family conversation and fireside dreaming may be found every recompense for the day's extra efforts and the rigid adherence to rules.

YOUR CUPBOARD:

The really efficient housewife opens the larder door to disclose rows of containers, each one neatly labeled to show its contents. The inefficient will be given away by untidy groups of grocery bags and wrappers piled any old how on the shelves

Nobody can afford a disorderly cupboard nowadays; it wastes both time and foodstuffs. There should be glass or metal containers for everything; there is no need to spend money on standard types if you don't wish to—jam-jars, sweet or biscuit tins and similar alternatives make quite good substitutes. Labels and covers for everything; grease-proof paper and elastic bands, if nothing else. Get "him" to fit a high, narrow shelf at the back for "tinies"—spices, flavourings, etc. Everything scrupulously clean; a place for everything and everything in its place. Have a complete list of your larder needs to be tacked inside the cupboard door—to be consulted every day before you set out to do your shopping. A larder notebook in which to note the commodities you find running low. Believe me, such a

ANN HATHAWAY

cupboard will repay an hour's planning.

THE HOMECRAFT BOOK

The Work Of The House

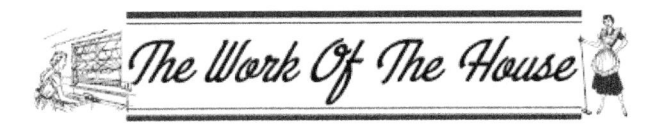

WEEKLY CLEANING: This should not be a heavy task, even to the single-handed housewife. Sweep and dust every room in use thoroughly every day. Every Friday clean silver, copper and brass articles, light-bulbs and insides of windows. On Mondays wash out any mats, etc., and iron them. At the beginning of each month polish all furniture. As soon as you see any marks on furniture or stains on rugs or upholstery, etc., remove them. Brush down the walls and ceilings every month and re-stain floor boards when they require it. The result of keeping a house clean in this way is that when spring arrives all the spring cleaning you will have to do will be to send your heavy curtains, and perhaps some rugs, to the cleaners to be cleaned.

SPRING CLEANING (To Plan): First have all the necessary repairs done to the house. Next, working on one room at a time, proceed as follows: (1) Take down all the soft furnishings, shake and send to laundry or cleaners, or wash and clean at home. (2) Pack all pictures and odds and ends out of the way. (3) Vacuum and roll up rugs and carpets and put them away, unless they are to go to the cleaners. (4) Cover up the furniture with dust sheets. Have the chimney swept if you have had fires, and clean the grate. (5) Now have decorations done, if any. If not, vacuum the walls, floors and ceilings. Then clean all woodwork, polish furniture and floors. Remove and vacuum books, clean bedding and turn out drawers and cupboards. (6) Replace carpets which you have cleaned and repaired elsewhere. Clean and replace all ornaments, fittings and utensils.

CLEANING UP AFTER MEALS: (1) Remove cruets or salt and pepper castors. Refill when necessary and polish. (2) Wash and dry mustard spoons, and any spoons or forks used for pickles or preserves. (3) Empty dishes containing preserves, wash and dry. If they are fitted with covers refill and cover. (4) Remove any bones or scrap from plates, wipe greasy plates and dishes with paper, burn the paper. Stack plates for washing, place left-over meat etc., under a cover in the larder. (5) Place left-over joint on a clean dish under cover in larder. (If any meat essence or gravy remains on the dish, rinse with boiling water into stock pot). (6) Drain off tea and burn tea leaves, coffee-grounds, and any scraps of vegetables unfit for food. If you attend to the first three points, table-setting will be simple. If you attend to the fourth, dish-washing will be easy. If you attend to the fifth part, joint will be ready to serve cold. If you attend to the sixth your dustbin will smell all the sweeter, in the hot weather in particular. The more refuse you burn the better.

LABOUR-SAVING HINTS: Go over every inch of your home and remove ornaments or any article you can manage without. Line all your cupboards and kitchen shelves with American cloth; this only needs a wipe down. Make bathroom, kitchen, and even bedroom curtains in oil baize; you can also use this cloth for kitchen cushions, tea cosy and aprons. Have glass and china finger plates put on all doors to prevent finger marks. Have all your brass fittings lacquered or chromium plated. Rub the windows after cleaning with a rag moistened with glycerine, which prevents steaming. Have a small table in your kitchen for family meals if you are a single-handed housekeeper. Spread paper on the kitchen table when working, also on any part of floor likely to be soiled.

Paint your cork table mats with enamel, cheerful and easy to keep clean.

Use two dusters at the same time—one in each hand when dusting your rooms. You'll find you can do your work much more quickly.

You can cut down the scrubbing jobs in your house by applying varnish to all plain wood objects you can find.

KITCHEN HINTS

KITCHEN TOWELS: When cotton shirts are past mending cut out the best parts, hem round and hang them near the sink. They are handy to wipe your hands on after washing up and save wear and tear on your kitchen towels.

LABELS (To prevent coming off): To save trouble of renewing labels which invariably come off when washing the glass and stone jars in which dry stores are kept; paint the labels over with glue size and then, when dry, give a coating of clear nail varnish. When treated in this way the labels do not wash off, and keep clean and fresh.

LABELLING TINS AND BOTTLES FOR THE KITCHEN: It is often found that the heat of the kitchen dries the labels off very quickly. To avoid this, wipe the back of the label with glycerine instead of water and it will be found that the labels adhere more securely.

FLAKING (To prevent): Enamelware is much less liable to flake if, before bringing into regular use, the vessel is filled with cold water, slowly brought to the boil and then left with the heat applied for a quarter of an hour. The water is then allowed to cool down and the vessel to become cold.

FUR (To prevent forming): A small stone marble kept inside a kettle will prevent fur forming.

FUR (Extermination): One tablespoon of borax put into an ordinary large kettleful of water, brought to the boil and the process repeated until the "fur" has vanished.

SMELL OF COOKING (To rid the house of): If the smell of cooking has pervaded the house, a bowl of water with a few drops of oil of lavender or lavender water poured into it and stood on the stove will soon drive out the smell.

BLACK-LEADING TIP: After black-leading a stove, polish with wax and it will only need dusting for a long time.

KITCHEN SLATE: Keep a slate and pencil in your kitchen and when household articles become used up or nearly so, just jot it down on your slate. This will save endless worry when the weekly order has to be made out for the grocer, baker, butcher, etc.

WASHING UP

WHEN WASHING POTS OR PANS: After cooking onions, always wash in cold water first to take away the smell. Then in hot water with some washing mixture added.

WASHING GLASSES: Glasses should be washed in hot water and dry soap, rinsed under the hot tap, on no account wiped. You will find that if the glasses are simply placed to drain they will dry off with a brighter polish than if they were laboriously wiped with a wet cloth and dish cloth.

SILVER need not be cleaned with anything like the same frequency if put straight into the sink and covered with boiling water with a little dry soap added.

HARDENED PIECES OF FOOD OR CRUST (To remove off plates or dishes when washing up): Sew an ordinary bone button to one corner of your dish cloth: it makes a very efficient scrape.

SAUCEPAN CLEANERS will last longer if a piece of cloth is tied around when scouring.

ATER BOILING MILK: Turn the pan upside down—

CHINA

TO REPAIR CHINA: For repairing china and filing small holes, cracks, etc., take a lump of quicklime and reduce it to a fine powder; then add a portion of the white of an egg to it and mix the paste to a creamy thickness; mix well with a knife and quickly apply the paste to the damaged parts, smoothing it on the outside with the knife after the crack has been well filled in and pressed to make the cake solid. It will set as hard as the china itself.

DOUBLE LIFE OF NEW CUPS AND SAUCERS: If you want to double the life of your crockery, put every piece as you but it in a pan of cold water and bring it slowly to the boil. Leave it until the water cools.

TINY CRACKS IN CHINA: Tiny cracks sometimes mar the appearance of one or more pieces in a favourite set of china. These cracks will disappear if the article is brought *very slowly* to the boil in milk and allowed to boil for a few minutes.

POURING BOILING WATER INTO CHINA: When pouring boiling water into glass or delphware, always place a spoon standing upright in the same. The spoon attracts the heat and prevents jug or glass from being cracked.

CEMENT FOR CHINA: Common alum makes quite a good cement for china, melt it in a spoon over the gas and apply while hot.

A very small amount of white of egg mixed thoroughly with lime and applied quickly will cement broken crockery.

BROKEN (Use for): Broken china makes an excellent knife sharpener, so before throwing away the smashed pieces, sharpen the kitchen knives along the edges.

TO PREVENT BREAKAGES: Cover your kitchen taps with adhesive tape, this will prevent breakages; cups and saucers are so often knocked accidently against the taps and get chipped or broken.

FRAGILE CHINA (To wash): China, no matter how fragile can be washed in warm water and Fuller's earth.

FURNITURE

HOT PLATE MARKS ON POLISHED TABLE: These may be obliterated in the following manner: First rub the mark thoroughly with linseed oil; then with a soft rag which has been dipped in the spirits of camphor go over the place lightly. Repeat the work until the mark of the plates disappear.

TO PROTECT POLISHED SURFACE: The surfaces of tables, bookcases, etc., are frequently marked by the feet of ornaments and flower vases. Cut out pieces of thick blotting paper exactly the same size and shape as the base of the vases and place them underneath. These will not show and will prevent scratching and marks from the moisture on the vases.

SCRATCHES ON FURNITURE: These can be removed by leaving a cloth soaked in linseed oil over the scratched part for an hour or so, then at once rubbing the place well with furniture polish.

CASTOR OIL FOR LEATHER CHAIRS: Leather chairs which are kept near the fire, or leather-upholstered fender will say "thank you" for a good rub of castor oil. Leave for three hours or so to soak in and then polish with a dry duster. This will stop the leather from cracking.

EASING DRAWER: If a drawer pulls in and out with difficulty, rub the smooth sides with furniture polish two or three times at intervals and shine them. It is surprising how easily the will run after this treatment. Do not apply a great deal of polish but give plenty of rubbing.

HEAT MARKS: Camphorated oil will darken and help to conceal heat marks on polished wood.

POLISHNG: (1) Try wringing out a flannel nearly dry in warm water before applying polish to furniture with it; you save labour in rubbing and get a high shine without smearing; polish as usual with a dry, soft duster afterwards.

(2) Wipe furniture with a leather wrung out of cold water, to which has been added a little vinegar, before using furniture polish; it will then shine readily.

REMOVE DUST: Try using a paint brush instead of an ordinary duster when dusting carved furniture; you will find that the brush can get into all crevices.

LIQUID FURNITURE POLISH: Equal quantities of linseed oil and turpentine; half quantities of methylated spirit and vinegar. Method: Put these into a bottle, cork and shake before using.

CARPETS

WORN (To dye): When carpet is worn and pile off, get a small packet of dye the colour that is most predominant in the carpet and make a strong solution by mixing it in hot water, apply to worn parts with a small brush and let it dry, or you can darn worn parts like a sock and paint with dye.

TO FRESHEN CARPETS: Sponge with strong salt water or brush with a broom dipped in warm water mixed with a little spirits of turpentine.

TO BEAT: Do not beat carpets with a stick as this tears the frill and tends to make them wear away in streaks. Hang them on the clothes line and beat with a proper carpet beater.

LINOLEUM

YOUR LINOLEUM: Once linoleum has had a couple of thorough applications of any good wax polish it is very easy to keep clean. A very good surface should be retained by an occasional sparing application of polish—once a week in the kitchen, etc., but bedrooms less often. Spare the polish. Too much gives the linoleum a greasy look, holds the dirt and makes the floor slippery. As little as possible and rub it in thoroughly. Daily attention with a soft broom and a quick polish with a dry or slightly oiled mop will keep it looking good. A damp cloth will remove footmarks, etc. Given this care it will rarely need washing or scrubbing. If you feel you must wash it, use warm soapy water and dry with a soft cloth. Above all, avoid the use of soda or any strong scouring soap; these remove the oil, spoil the surface and damage the cork substance. Finally, avoid polishing under mats.

ODD PIECES (To make use of): If you have any odd bits of lino, cut out nice round or oblong dish mats; put on a coat of lino paint and bind the edges with coloured beads and you have a most serviceable dish mat.

TO CLEAN: Use a loofah for scrubbing your linoleum; it cleans just as well as a brush and won't wear away the pattern.

HOT-WATER BOTTLES

CARE OF YOUR HOT-WATER BOTTLE: Wash your hot-water bottle out now and again with hot water and a spoonful of ammonia to keep it supple. Blow into it and put in the stopper when not in use to prevent the insides sticking together. A small leak can often be repaired by touching the spot with a red hot skewer so that the surrounding rubber melts a little and covers the hole; an even better way of course; is to use a cycle repair outfit patch, sticking it on just as you would for an inner tube, following the directions carefully. If the washer is at fault make a new one by cutting off the loop that hangs the bottle up and using that in place of the worn washer.

USING TO BEST ADVANTAGE: When using a hot water bottle for warming a bed, place it upright between the sheets; this allows the heat to spread, instead of being concentrated at one spot.

TO PREVENT RUBBER HOT-WATER JARS FROM BURSTING: Add a few drops of cold water first, even boiling water can then be added without fear of burst. Always fill jar lying flat, this prevents water bubbling up and helps to avoid scalds, etc. Cork jar in that position: it helps to keep out air.

UMBRELLAS

TO REPAIR: Sometimes a good cover breaks away or ravels at the point of the ribs. If the umbrella is black this can be made good by stitching small pieces from the tops of black soles or stockings on to the frayed part. Small holes can also be mended the same way, putting the patch inside; this material gives when the umbrella is opened.

TORN: A neat way to mend a torn umbrella, if the rent is not large, is to stitch firmly a piece of black court plaster on the inside. This does not show nearly as much as a darn.

TREATMENT WHEN WET: Wet umbrella should not be stood point downwards in the stand; the wires will rust and the silk will rot. Nor should they be opened wide and left to dry; this will stretch the covering and make it loose. The best plan is to shake the umbrella free of water and then stand it, half or nearly open on the handle. If the frame will not stay half open, keep it in the required position with a rubber band slipped up the handle.

TO PREVENT UMBRELLA FRAMES FROM RUSTING: Rub a small quantity of Vaseline over each hinge in the frame. This will not soil the cover and will prolong the life of the umbrella.

UMBRELLA (Re-proof): To re-proof worn umbrella make a solution of three dessertspoonfuls of powdered alum to one pint of cold water. Wet umbrella thoroughly, using a piece of material the same colour as the umbrella to apply. Leave open to dry slowly and you will find it quite serviceable.

A SHABBY UMBRELLA: A shabby umbrella can be renovated by brushing with a solution of ammonia and warm water.

TO REVIVE AN UMBRELLA that has seen too many rainy days: Mix a tablespoonful of sugar with half a pint of boiling water. Sponge the umbrella carefully and then hang up outside to dry.

TO CLEAN

BATHS: These are usually of porcelain or enameled iron. Care should be taken to prevent the surface being scratched or damaged, so gritty abrasives must be avoided. There are several good cleaners obtainable. Daily cleaning makes the weekly cleaning much easier. Other points to remember:

(1) TURN ON COLD WATER FIRST; particularly if it is an enameled bath. If porcelain, very hot water may cause cracking;

(2) Train the family to remove "high water" marks—see that there is a cloth handy for this;

(3) If taps drip, have them seen to or the bath will become discoloured with rust marks;

SINKS: (1) The sink should be given a daily cleansing. After the principal meal's washing up, scrub with hot, soapy water and a cleaning powder. Place a little soda on the opening to the drain and pour down a kettleful of boiling water. Flush with clean cold water. *Remember* to pour dirty and greasy water away outside;

(2) A sink basket should be provided;

(3) A skewer is useful for cleaning the grating;

(4) Disinfect regularly;

(5) If the plug is a rubber one, clean occasionally with a rag damped with turpentine.

PAINTWORK: It helps to keep woodwork bright and fresh if you wipe it over with a soft rag dipped in warm, soapy water, but to do this too often is likely to dull the high glossy finish which is so admired in paintwork. Here is a suggestion for putting a polish to paint: Melt a few tablespoonfuls of painter's size in boiling water, and when cool soak a cloth in the solution, wring most of it out and then go over and clean the paintwork. When dry, it looks as if the paint has had a fresh coat of varnish.

OVENS: Oven-cleaning can be very easy if, when the oven is thoroughly clean, a stiff brush is dipped into hot water, then into scouring powder, which is brushed well over the oven and left to dry. Wash off with hot water and repeat the process. If possible the oven should be hot, when it will be found that the method of cleaning is both quick and effective.

YELLOWED BONE KNIFE HANDLES (To bleach): Rub with a flannel soaked in peroxide of hydrogen or by standing them, handles down in a jar of peroxide and water.

TILES: Instead of washing your tiles try using a chamois leather wrung out of water: clean them with it in exactly the same way as you would a window. Polish with a clean, warm duster and the tiles will be shining, with no dirt or smears on them.

RUSTY CURTAIN HOOKS: When curtain hooks become rusty and stick instead of gliding easily along with the curtains they should be cleaned thoroughly in ammonia. Put curtains hooks in a jar completely covered with cloudy ammonia and leave them to soak for about three-quarters of an hour, stirring them round occasionally. After this treatment the hooks will have lost any signs of rust and become equal to new again.

SILVER: (1) The filmy, broken powder caused by the breaking of an incandescent gas mantle will clean silverware if rubbed on with a soft cloth. Polish afterwards with another clean duster. It may not remove bad stains but it gives a beautiful gloss to forks and spoons;

(2) Mix equal quantities of liquid ammonia and water, stir in enough whiting to make it milky and pour this into a bottle to store...Use for embossed and engraved silver articles which would be made unsightly by white deposits, if ordinary metal polish or plate powder were used.

VACUUM FLASKS: When washing, add a little vinegar to water. It will help to clean a flask and remove any musty smell. If the flask is badly stained, add a crushed egg shell to the vinegar and water and shake vigorously for a few minutes. Then leave the mixture to stand for a short time.

PAINTED WALLS: To clean washable painted walls or distempered walls, dip a cloth damped with warm water into common baking soda and rub it on. Do a small piece at a time and finish by wiping the whole wall with a clean, wet cloth.

PIANO KEYS: Wash with warm water and borax (1 teaspoon to a pint). If they have become yellow and discoloured thorough washing with soap and water, apply a thin cream of whiting and turpentine; leave this to dry on and polish well.

FELT HATS: Rain-spotted felt hats can be put right again by passing spotted part to and fro in front of the spout of a fast-boiling kettle. Dry in front of the fire and brush carefully with a soft brush.

DRY CLEANING WINDOWS AND MIRRORS: Make an envelope of thick flannelette big enough to fit comfortably in the hand; fill it with whiting and fold over and stitch the open end. Rub over the window or mirror with the pad and polish with a clean soft duster.

VARNISHED WALLPAPER: Varnished wallpaper which has been splashed with grease from the stove can be washed with a pailful of warm soapy water to which a tablespoonful of ammonia has been added.

ALLUMINIUM WARE: Save some ashes when cleaning out the grate, pass them through a sieve and use them to scour the pans, inside and out. Then wash with warm soapy water.

PACK OF CARDS: Spread cards on the table, sprinkle them generously with talcum powder and then shuffle them; or you can also clean very soiled or greasy cards by rubbing them lightly with a clean rag or piece of cotton wool dipped in Eau-de-Cologne.

DIAMOND RING: An easy way to clean a diamond ring is to place it in an egg cup with a little Eau-de-Cologne and leave for a few minutes. When the ring is taken out it will be seen that all the particles of dust are left at the bottom of the egg cup. When perfectly dry, brush off lightly with a clean brush and no marks will remain.

WINDOWS: Get half a dozen leaves of rhubarb, chop them up, put into a saucepan, add 1 pint of water, simmer for 3 hours, then strain off the liquid; put in a tablespoonful of whiting and mix to a cream.

CLOUDY DECANTER: (1) Light a piece of brown paper and put it inside the bottle, hold your hand over the opening until the decanter is filled with smoke. Rinse decanter well and you will find it perfectly clear;

(2) To clean a decanter put small pieces of potato into it and equal parts of vinegar and water. Shake well for a few minutes.

NECKLACES (Pearl): To clean a pearl necklace, submerge it in a small tin of powdered magnesia, leave for a night, and gently brush powder off in the morning.

EGG SPOONS: If egg spoons are dipped in very hot water and then wiped with a cold wet cloth, the egg which clings so obstinately comes away without any trouble.

SAUCEPAN (Burnt): If a saucepan becomes burnt, simply fill it with salt water and leave for twenty-four hours. It can then be readily cleaned.

GAS OVENS: To clean inside them pour a little vinegar into one saucepan and a handful of common salt into another. Dip a piece of flannel alternately into the vinegar and salt and rub the sides and the door of the oven. Do this when the oven is warm.

BAKELITE ARTICLES: These sometimes need special cleaning and you will find that ordinary metal polish cleans them well. Use in the usual way, then wash the article in lukewarm soapy water. Dry on a soft cloth.

LAMPS: Clean lamps early in the day, then turn wick down. If not cleaned daily the flame may dance and flicker. Keep burner very clean, rubbing off burnt oil with emery from time to time.

PAPIER MACHÉ: Wash in warm water with a little soap jelly dissolved in it, then dry and rub with a little sweet oil. If you want it highly polished apply a little wax polish and rub with a silk duster.

BLACK FELT HAT: Brush the hat free of dust, then add a tablespoonful of strong ammonia to five tablespoonfuls of cold tea, and clean the surface by rubbing it thoroughly with a clean cloth dipped in this mixture.

SLIMY SPONGES: Soak in strong vinegar and water for half an hour. Wash out in warm water and rinse in cold. Hang in a draught to dry, preferably in the open.

FACE CLOTHS: These can be kept sweet and fresh by washing and boiling them in vinegar and water.

TILED FLOORS: Try boiled linseed oil for tiled floors; apply it on a soft woollen cloth instead of scrubbing.

BADLY STAINED STEEL KNIVES: Badly stained steel knives can be cleaned swiftly with a slice of raw potato dipped in powdered bathbrick.

EYE GLASSES: To make eye glasses really beautifully clear, clean with methylated spirits. Dry and polish with a chamois leather.

CELLULOID ARTICLES: Clean the same way as metal ones—by using metal polish.

CHIMNEY: A piece of zinc burned with your turf will free your chimney from soot.

GILT PICTURE FRAMES: (1) Wash gently with water in which onions have been boiled. Use a very soft cloth, or a sponge, both for washing and for drying. Don't make them very wet.

ALUMINIUM: Aluminium may be given a brilliant polish by rubbing with methylated spirit and whiting.

BLACKLEAD AND SHOE BRUSHES: Wash in strong hot soda water.

FIBRE SUITCASES: Clean by sponging them with hot vinegar and water then polish with floor polish.

DISCOLOURED BRASS RODS: Clean with paste of turpentine and powdered pumice; then polish with metal polish.

VARNISHED PAPERS: Cleaned with a solution of

paraffin and water. Then, afterwards, shine with a soft cloth.

GREASY ALUMINIUM: Powdered pumice is excellent for removing grease from aluminium.

CREAM LINEN BLINDS: Place them on a table and scrub with a clean, dry nail brush dipped in powdered bathbrick. Afterwards dust over with a clean duster.

PLUSH CURTAINS: Hot salt rubbed hard into plush curtains is the best way to dry clean them.

BORAX AS A CLEANSER: Borax is excellent for cleaning copper, cleansing table-ware and sweetening tea and coffee pots.

GRATES: Some methylated spirit added to blacklead will give a grate a gloss like enamel.

PLATE: Wash plate in hot, soapy water to which a few drops of ammonia has been added, dry and polish with a chamois leather.

A COPPER KETTLE: Fill with hot water and polish outside with a rag dipped in buttermilk or sour milk, or rub with equal quantities of salt and vinegar. Wash off with soapy water. Rinse in warm water and polish with a soft cloth.

TEAPOT: To clean a teapot: Boil one teaspoonful of pearl barley in a little water. Pour into teapot and leave over-night.

CHROMIUM FITTINGS: Don't weary yourself trying to keep your chromium fittings bright, apply a little floor polish, shine in the usual way and you have a lasting brightness.

CANE OR WICKER CHAIRS: Well brush cane or wicker chairs, then wash with warm water and salt.

RUBBER MATS: Rubber mats, if constantly washed, seem to acquire quite a "bloom" but you can soon give them a nice gloss and again by giving them a good brushing with an ordinary shoe cream. Apply the cream with a soft brush, then give a final rub with an old rag.

TO MEND

ZINC PAILS: To mend zinc pails and enamelware place a small piece of putty on the inside of the hole and a large piece on the outside, press the putty down well and stand in the open air till the putty is quite hard when the pail will hold water and be as good as ever.

Enamel bowls, etc., can be mended the same way and a small quantity will mend several.

WELLINGTON BOOTS: Wellington boots, hot-water bottles and rubber household gloves can all be mended if you buy a small bicycle puncture outfit. In the case of wellington boots, paint the patch when fixed with enamel to match the boot.

KNIVES: Sealing wax will mend knives whose blades and handles have parted company. Fill the hole in the middle with sealing wax, heat the pointed hasp of the knife over a gas jet and plunge it into the wax, pushing it, as it meets the wax, right home and hold it in position for a few minutes.

AN IRON SAUCEPAN: Use two parts sulphur to one part fine blacklead. Melt sulphur in old iron pot on stove and when melted, add blacklead, and mix gently; leave on iron plate to cool and harden. Break off piece and put on crack or hole in pan, working it well in with hot soldering iron.

A PAIL: If you have a pail which has developed small holes in the bottom, turn it upside down and give the underside a good coat of enamel. While the paint is still wet spread a piece of calico smoothly over it. Allow the paint and calico to dry together, then give a second coat of enamel over the material. When the second coat of enamel is dry, the pail is ready again for use.

A SAUCEPAN: Mend a hole in a saucepan or baking tin by putting the point of a drawing pin through the hole from the outside and hammering the point down flat on the inside.

LOOSE TILES: (1) Mix four parts of ordinary whiting

with one part liquid waterglass as used for preserving eggs. Thus you have a quick-hardening cement, which is waterproof. It can be polished to a white finish. For holding tiles in position it is superior to any cement sold to-day;

(2) A loose tile in the hearth or wherever damp does not exist may be fixed firmly by smearing the back with liquid glue and pressing down with force.

KITCHEN KNIFE: When the kitchen knife parts company with its handle, clean out the hole, fill it with powdered resin, then clean the tang (the pointed part of the blade) hold over a flame and press into the resin. It will set hard.

CEILINGS THAT FLAKE: If a ceiling becomes flaky and portions of the whitewash tend to fall away, make a solution of alum (½ oz.) and water (1 pint). Paint this on the ceiling with a soft brush.

LACE AND NET CURTAINS: When torn, these need not be darned, or caught up when in holes. Wash and starch them as usual and, when ironing, cut a circle out of an old curtain, dip it in starch, and iron over the hole. This makes an admirable match, and the time taken is negligible.

PATCH YOUR LINOLEUM: By filling in the holes made by chair castors or old age with whiting and linseed oil mixed to a stiff putty; press it well in: smooth with a knife and when dry and hard, colour to match the surrounding linoleum.

JEWELLERY: Little pieces of decorative jewellery that get broken can often be mended very satisfactorily with a little colourless nail varnish.

STONE HOT-WATER BOTTLE: Mend a cracked stone hot-water bottle by heating well, painting outside of crack with neat waterglass, putting in stopper at once and leaving for twelve hours: as air cools inside, the waterglass seals the crack.

BUCKET: Mend a hole in a bucket or bath by filling

with putty and leaving to dry naturally for several days.

RUBBER HOT-WATER BOTTLES: A tiny hole or a small part of a hot-water bottle which has become porous may be mended by putting a piece of sticking-plaster over it.

LEAKING PIPE: (1) Bind leaking pipe with adhesive tape while waiting for plumber;

(2) Soap mixed with whiting will stop a leaking water pipe until the plumber comes.

MENDING FURNITURE: A loose chair leg can be made quite firm by fixing two angle brackets to the leg and underside of the seat frame. Angle brackets about 2 ins. in size are needed, and the necessary screws for fixing. Turn the chair upside down on a table and place the brackets in position, making quite sure the leg is straight. Mark the positions for the screws by penciling through the screw holes, then make the holes, first with a bradawl. Put the brackets in position again and screw up lightly. Now turn the chair on its legs to make sure they are even before tightening up brackets.

NAIL-HOLES IN WALL (To repair): A paste of ordinary whiting and milk, formed into a thick pellet and pressed into nail-holes in walls will set hard as mortar and can be easily painted or distempered over.

Household Hints

RUBBER ARTICLES THAT HAVE BECOME HARD: If you find that last year's rubber bathing cap, sponge bag, beach shoes or other bathing paraphernalia had gone hard during winter storage, don't be dismayed: here is a simple way of putting things right again: Make a solution of one part liquid ammonia to two parts of cold water and soak the stiffened rubber articles in it for a few minutes or a few hours, it all depends on how bad they are; find out when treatment has taken effect by testing the rubber with your hands.

HOT LIQUIDS: If you have to pour a very hot liquid into a glass or bottle and there is a fear of cracking it, stand the vessel on a cloth that is quite wet. It is almost certain that no damage will be done to the vessel.

NON-RUSTING CURTAIN PINS: If curtain pins are dipped in white enamel before use this will prevent rust marks on curtains.

A BROOM HOLDER: Brooms should never be left standing in a cupboard with the head resting on the floor. This soon impairs the bristles. Drive two long nails into the wall, about two inches apart and let the broom head rest on these, the handle downwards.

YOUR OWN TAPE MEASURE: When there is no tape-measure or ruler available, remember this little list of approximate lengths—I have found it invaluable in emergencies:

>One sixpence—three-quarters of an inch.
>
>Five pennies—six inches.
>
>The nail-joint of first finger—one inch.
>
>Span of thumb and index finger—seven inches.
>
>Span of thumb and little finger—nine inches.
>
>Wrist to elbow—ten inches.

RAZOR BLADES (To prevent going rusty): To prevent razor blades from going rusty keep them between a fold of blotting-paper after use. You could make a book of blotting-paper pages and give it to your husband for this purpose.

HOME-MADE METAL POLISH: Mix half cup of powdered whiting with half cup of cold water, pour it into a bottle, add one ounce of ammonia and shake well before using to polish brass or silver.

WHEN TUMBLERS GET STRUCK TOGETHER: A very simple way of separating them is to fill the upper glass with cold water, which will allow it to contract, and dip the lower one in warm water, which will cause it to expand. The glasses can then be easily parted.

RE-PAPERING OVER DAMP PATCHES: Before re-papering a room or a cupboard, give the bare walls, where dampness has appeared, three coats of waterglass, the same as is used for preserving eggs. Be sure that each coating is dry before another is applied. Dampness will never penetrate after this treatment.

TO CLEAR SCULLERY PIPE: If the scullery sink has become clogged, fill the sink three-parts with water, then put a rubber ball over the exit and press on it several times smartly. This will clear the pipe.

TO RESTORE CRUSHED BRISTLES IN BROOMS: Half fill a kettle with water and bring to the boil. When the steam is pouring steadily from the sprout, hold the crushed broom to it. Rub the hand smartly over the bristles, taking care not to let it approach too near the scalding steam.

This treatment restores both bristle and fibre brushes.

CUT FLOWERS: In hot weather, use jars rather than glasses because the water will then be kept cooler. Snip a little piece off the end of each stalk daily when changing the water. Do not leave costly blooms in hot rooms at night; put them in a cool place.

BASKETS (To preserve): If baskets are occasionally scrubbed with hot soap suds they will last much longer.

SAVE PAPER: Hem some butter muslin in squares and use them instead of paper to wrap up sandwiches and other foods for carried lunches. The muslin is easily washed and kept clean. Bags of the same material would be useful in your shopping bag and save paper.

BATHROOM MIRRORS STEAMING UP (To prevent): Rub over with piece of almost dry soap. Then polish with soft duster till clear.

CELLOPHANE SCRAPS: Scraps of cellophane make excellent covers for books, keeping them clean and allowing the title to be easily seen.

ACID FROM ACCUMULATORS: If acid from your wireless accumulator gets spilt on a carpet apply liquid ammonia to the spots at once. This neutralizes the acid and prevents it burning holes in the material.

OIL OF LAVENDER gives such a fresh perfume that it is liked by almost everyone. A few drops can be laid inside drawers and cupboards to give them a fresh smell.

NEW LIFE FOR OLD BRUSHES: To give a new lease of life to any old brushes (hair, tooth, clothes, scrubbing that have lost their springiness, dissolve twopennyworth of alum in a quart of boiling water. Wash the brushes in the usual way, then steep them to the ends of the bristles in the alum solution. Leave them to soak for about three hours, then remove from the solution, shake off any surplus moisture and dry them in the open air. The bristles will seem like new.

MUSTINESS IN SILVER TEAPOT (To prevent): Keep some unused tea leaves in the silver teapot when it is not in daily use. This does away with any mustiness and when the pot is brought to the table, the flavour of the tea is not spoiled.

STALE TOBACCO FUMES (To rid a room of): Put a lump of rock ammonia into a bowl with a few drops of oil of lavender. Then pour over it about a cupful of boiling water and allow it to stand in the room until cold.

SASH CORDS (To lengthen the life of): Rub cords, occasionally with melted candle grease or soap.

GAY BOOKS BRIGHTEN A ROOM: Restore canvas or linen covers by wringing a cloth out of hot water, rubbing the cover briskly all over and then drying with another cloth at once.

BABY'S PRAM HOOD: The sun can do a lot of damage to the hood of a pram, so give it a rub over every day with a cloth soaked in olive oil.

A DOOR OR WINDOW WHICH STICKS: If you have a door or window which sticks, rub the parts marked by tightness with an ordinary candle. You won't be troubled any more.

TIGHT JAR-LIDS (To unscrew): Keep a piece of sandpaper handy in the kitchen cabinet.

MUSTINESS IN VACUUM FLASK (To prevent): Do not cork a vacuum flask when putting it away or it will develop a musty odour.

GUMMED LABELS: If gummed labels, postage stamps or jam-pot covers have become glued together, do not soak in water, but lay a thin paper over them and pass a hot iron over. They will come apart easily and gum will be intact.

SAUCEPAN CLEANER: Make a saucepan cleaner from a string and wire. Knit the string and wire into a ten-inch square.

DULL FIRE (To re-light): Don't despair when the fire goes dull; place a cork on the hot ashes, light it, and the fire will glow.

PAINTED OR NEWLY-VARNISHED DOORS (To

preserve): Cut out cardboard to fit around any brass fittings and use when cleaning same with metal polish.

MINCING MACHINE (To sharpen): When mincing machines go dull and don't mince the way they should, run through a little crumbled-up bathbrick and then wash out well.

SALT GOING DAMP (To prevent): A dry pea in a salt-shaker keeps the salt from becoming lumpy and damp; renew the pea when necessary.

POTATO (Uses for): (1) A good use for the humble potato is to rub it over grates, etc., before applying blacklead and the shine will last much longer;

(2) A strong, quickly-made glue is made by rubbing a little piece of cold, boiled potato on a sheet of paper with the fingers.

RUBBER SPONGES (Care of): Remember that rubber sponges will soon perish if left to dry with soap in them, so always rinse them thoroughly.

BATHROOM MATS THAT HAVE BECOME HARD: Bathroom mats of crepe rubber sometimes become hard and curl up at the ends in cold weather. This can be remedied by immersing the mats in warm water until they become soft again.

WET SHOES (To shine): A drop or two of paraffin added to boot polish will help to shine boots or shoes that have been soaked on a wet day.

WIRE MATTRESS (To clean): A bicycle pump is best for removing dust from a wire mattress or crevice that is hard to get at with a duster.

FLOWERS WITH SHORT STEMS: Short-stemmed flowers will stand erect and last much longer if arranged in a bowl filled with moistened sand or sifted earth.

Substitutes

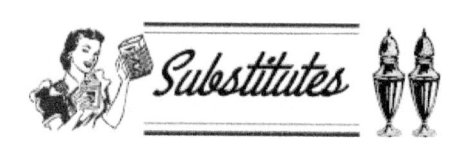

CEMENT: Cement is not always obtainable for household jobs so here is a substitute: Mix our parts of ordinary whiting with one part of liquid waterglass and you have a quick-drying cement which is waterproof and will hold loose tiles in position, mend pails, etc., and take the place of builder's cement.

SHEETS: Short of sheets? How about digging out those enormous white tablecloths of yesteryear—wash the starch out and there you are.

HANDLE OF SUITCASE: The broken handle of suitcase can be replaced with an ordinary dog collar; slip the collar through the two loops and buckle it to the right length.

SINK WASTE BASKET: An ordinary flower pot is a very good substitute for a waste basket. The hole at the bottom allows for drainage, and the pot takes up little space and can be easily cleaned or replaced.

VACUUM: If you haven't a vacuum cleaner, throw a wet sheet over your armchairs and beat them through the sheet with a carpet beater; the dust flies out and sticks to the wet sheet.

CASSEROLES (Makeshift for): An enamel pie dish covered with white paper which is pleated all around under the edge of the dish makes a good substitute for a casserole. Or you can use a 2 lb. jam jar with a saucer on top.

FLOOR POLISH: Wash and thoroughly dry your linoleum or oilcloth: make a little starch in a pint basin with boiling water and rub lightly over with a clean cloth. It will dry very brightly without any further rubbing or polishing and will be glossy but not slippy.

BLANKET: If your supply of blankets is limited, put a sheet between two blankets. This keeps the warmth in and is almost as warm as an extra blanket.

STARCH: (1) Borax can be used as a substitute for starch in stiffening fine materials;

(2) The water in which rice has been cooked makes quite a fair substitute for starch. Wash the rice extra well before boiling it.

BLUE-BAG: Put one tablespoonful of waterglasss to one gallon of water in your boiler. Boil in usual way. Keeps clothes perfectly white.

Uses For Old Articles

LINEN: No tiniest scrap of linen should be discarded as worthless. A good roll of old linen should be kept always in the linen closet for use in household emergencies. It should be wound into neat rolls and kept spotlessly fresh, so that the store can be called upon when burnt fingers or cut knees call for first-aid. A small bag of linen should be made in which small rolls can be kept. For kitchen use—a bag of scraps kept behind the kitchen door is invaluable. These serve as rubbers and kitchen cloths for innumerable purposes. The use of one or two, to be thrown away when soiled, is a great saving of the better type of duster and tea-towels.

VELVET: (1) If you have any pieces of old worn velvet tack it round the edges of your brooms, mops and carpet-sweepers. It stoops all those nasty scratches around the skirting boards and on the furniture;

(2) If you have a discarded velvet or velveteen dress or coat, you can make use of it for many things. Here are a few: Make pads for polishing furniture and grates; line inside bottom of hubby's trousers to prevent fraying; small pieces will do nicely pasted inside kiddies' shoes to prevent slipping up and down and wearing holes in socks. Buttons can also be covered.

SILK STOCKINGS make a useful cushion or quilt

filling if you cut off tops and feet, then catch a thread on the cut edge and pull it the stockings will unravel freely and provide a downy mass for filling.

TOWELS: From the least-worn parts make a pair of gloves in the shape of babies' gloves, with a stall for the thumb and all the fingers together in one stall. Next time you wash your hair slip your hands into these towel gloves when you are ready to dry it. Massage your head vigorously with your gloved hands and you will find that you will dry your hair far more easily than when you rub it with a towel.

FELT HAT: Take an old felt hat and cut out discs about the size of a sixpence or a shilling. Fasten these secure with gum or glue to the bottom of the legs of chairs, tables or other moveable articles not already provided with castors. This will also prevent scratched on polished floors and linoleum.

INTERLOCK VEST: If you have any old interlock vests or pants, cut them into long strips for bandages, As well as being very soft they will stretch and will not fray too badly. If you roll them up into different widths and put a rubber band round them, you will be pleasantly surprised how nice they are to use.

STIFF COLLARS that are frayed beyond repair can be cut up into excellent tie-on labels which will never tear. Make a hole about ¾ inch in from one end and thread a short length of string through this.

SUEDE GLOVES: Cut a strip and glue it to the inside of the heel of your shoe. The suede will grip and prevent wear on stockings.

BERET: Never discard your beret after it has served its purpose but thread a string through the double part of the rim and slip it over the head of your polishing mop. This new head will produce an excellent polish and when soiled can be removed and washed quite easily.

COTTON REELS make excellent doorstops or handles for small doors and drawers if a screw is put through the centre.

SOCKS: When socks cannot be repaired again, cut them to a convenient size and wear as knee pads to protect your stockings against ladders when kneeling, laying fires and other duties.

TORN RUBBER APRON: If you have an old torn rubber apron, cut an oval from the apron large enough to cover the top of your shopping basket. Always keep this inside the basket and then if it starts to rain just take the waterproof out and slip it over your packages.

PAIR OF FLANNEL TROUSERS can still be useful. Split one leg open and use to cover ironing board.

FELT WICKS: Felt makes excellent lamp wicks if cut with sharp scissors. It gives a clean edge and burns steadily.

WORN-OUT BROOMS: First burn away all the old bristles. Then find any old flannel or velvet you may have in your ragbag and bind the broomhead with this. Result: an excellent floor polisher.

TOOTH-BRUSHES (1) For cleaning silver, they get into the crevices; dusting the type-writer; cleaning round the base of awkward modern taps; cleaning hair-combs; scrubbing collars and cuffs; sandshoes and bicycle hubs.

(2) Keep that old, worn-out tooth-brush and use it for damping seams when you are pressing garments of thick material.

STRAINER: Here's a way of using up an old tea or coffee strainer: Use if for removing an egg from a saucepan of boiling water. The water drains away through the sieve immediately and causes no drops on the stove or floor.

PYJAMAS: The leg of old pyjama trousers makes an excellent top cover for an old ironing board and is easily removed for laundering.

COFFEE GROUNDS poured down the sink will prevent the pipe from blocking. They will also act as a deodorizer if burned in an unpleasant-smelling room.

CARPET: Treat old carpet the following way: Beat out all dust and lay it wrong side up, paint thinly with size and when dry give it two coats of paint or enamel. This "linoleum" will stand scrubbing and hard wear and will be warm to feet.

ALUMINIUM SAUCEPAN: Don't throw away aluminium saucepan because the handle is loose. Remove the handle and you have a nice tin for baking your cakes.

LAMPSHADES can be made to look like new if you find some gay-coloured wallpaper and paste on soiled covering, and when dry, paint over with some varnish.

CHAMOIS LEATHER is a wonderful heat holder: Line your tea cosy with patchwork pieces cut from old gloves and leathers.

PASTE JARS: Those small round jars in which you buy pastes, if thoroughly cleaned can be used as emergency egg-cups.

FELT: (1) Tack stripes of old felt along the base and side of a door; a neater, better draught excluder than the old-fashioned "sausage";

(2) In-soles for boots and shoes cut out from old felt hats are most comfortable.

KID GLOVES: The best patches for your son's elbows can be made from old kid gloves.

TENNIS RACKET: Do not throw away your old tennis racket, instead keep it for using a carpet beater, it will be most handy.

USED GRAMOPHONE NEEDLES serve excellently in place of brads for holding the backs of pictures, fixing linoleum, etc.

RAGS: Always keep a quantity of old rags in the peg basket. When hanging celanese garments they are invaluable: a small piece under each peg protects the garment from laddering.

MACKINTOSH: Cut out best part of old mack as a waterproof apron; very useful to wear under coat to keep front of skirt dry when cycling on wet day.

LINOLEUM: Lino firelighters: Cut old, discarded lino in strips with sharp knife, use these instead of sticks to light fires.

Waste Not - Want Not

CANDLE ENDS: Here is a way of using up old candle ends: Collect them till you have a good supply and then melt them down. Put the melted wax in a saucer and make tapers from it by drawing short lengths of fairly long string through it. Leave the wax string to set and you will have some tapers all ready to stand in a jar in your fireplace for people to use when lighting cigarettes. Such a saving on matches, too!

CORKS AND TINS (Uses for): Save corks of every size, and condensed milk tins. You can make your own stoppers for holes in enamelware. Slice corks with a razor blade, burn a hole through the centre with an old knitting needle; cut the tin with an old scissors; punch hole through centre with a nail; you can buy the small nuts and bolts in position. You have them for a half-penny each.

STRING (To use pieces of): Save all pieces if string, knot them together and wind in a ball. Get a pair of No. 9 steel needles, cast on 40 stitches and knit plain a piece of twelve or fifteen inches square. These make excellent dish cloths.

EGG WATER (A use for): Don't throw away the water in which eggs are boiled. It can be very useful. Steep the eggspoons in it and the stains which the eggs leave can soon be cleaned off. Or have you weeds in your garden? Well the water in which eggs have been boiled is a most effective weed-killer.

LABEL ECONOMY: If you have to use a tie-on label for luggage or parcel, write the address across the end, not down the whole length. Next time the label is needed cut this end off and write on the remaining piece.

SOAP SUDS (Use for): Never waste soap suds, no matter how dirty they are; throw them on rose trees and fruit bushes. In these days, when manures and fertilizers are short, they work wonders

TOOTH PASTE CAP (Use for): Use that Bakelite tooth paste cap to save soap; press it into the underside of a cake of soap so that it lifts the soap out of any dampness on the dish.

CANDLE-ENDS (To use): (1) Put a penny over the hole in candle-stick and stand the candle on it. It will burn to the last bit;

(2) A small piece of candle can be made burn all night by putting finely powdered salt on it until it reaches the blanket part of the wick.

EGG SHELLS (Uses for): (1) Egg shells crushed into small bits and shaken well in water bottles, etc., three parts filled with cold water will not only clean them, but make the glass like new;

(2) In every household a number of eggs are used every day and usually the egg shells are thrown away as useless. Instead, they should be dried and crushed as finely as possible with the rolling pin. Use the powder for removing the stains on enamel saucepans, teapots and coffee pots, etc. Wring out a cloth in warm water, dip it in the egg shells and rub gently.

BLUE-WATER (To use up): Never throw blue-water down the sink; use it for scrubbing down your whitewood kitchen table, draining board, etc. It makes them twice as good looking.

GREASEPROOF PAPER (To renew): Wash greaseproof paper carefully, dry and iron and it will be good as new.

ODD TEAPOT LID: If you break a teapot, save the lid: it will make a handy cover for one of your jam jars in the store cupboard.

FULL ECONOMY

COAL DUST (To use up): If you have any coal dust, make it into briquettes now. Mix six parts of coal dust with one part damp clay or turf mould. Press into old flower pots or small boxes and leave in a dry shed for the winter.

FIRECLAY: Obtain a packet of fireclay. Mix it to a stiff paste with water, knead and shape into balls about the size of an orange. Dry in oven. When needed, place one or two in the fire. They become red hot, give out a great heat, and can be used over and over again.

SLACK (To use up): Mix two good buckets of slack with a bucket of ordinary garden earth. Use a little water and mix all with a shovel. From mixture into convenient-sized balls. Leave for a day or two to soak and harden off. These will make a grand fire.

SLACK (Substitute): Apple peel, rinds, or sinks of either fruit or vegetables make an excellent slack substitute. When placed on top of a turf or log fire, they retain the heat and make an excellent blaze.

SAVE GAS by putting your own baking sheet over the biggest gas ring turned on full; then several saucepans can be kept boiling at once.

SOAP ECONOMY

Buy one of these soap mats that hold the soap up out of the dish or press a crown bottle stopper into side of a new cake and always dry the soap before putting it back. As soon as you buy soap powder or flakes, decant it from the packet into the tin, and keep an old spoon or scoop in the tin, measure your flakes out, don't toss them in haphazardly. Use an old tin with a perforated lid for powders. Use rainwater as much as possible, it is so soft that a mere pinch of powder makes a splendid lather; the harder the water the more soap is required. Make soapy water do double duty; that used for washing through your undies is quite clean enough to scrub the floor.

SOAP SAVING: Washing of the hands may be accomplished in a new way. Rub the dry, dirty hands with the soap which probably is moist; use no water; lay the soap down and rub the hands well together, then wet them and continue rubbing, when a good lather is procured; after rinsing they will be perfectly clean. The soap, however, is not wet and will last much longer.

DON'T KEEP ON USING YOUR CAKE OF SOAP until it is so thin that it breaks into pieces—most of which will be lost down the drain. When the cake gets too thin to use comfortably, press it firmly on to the new cake. In this way not a bit of it will be lost or wasted.

SOAP JELLY: Save all remnants of soap in a jar. When a good collection has been made, cover with boiling water, stir well and leave until set. This jelly may be used for washing woolen articles with the addition of more soap or washing powder.

TOILET SOAP: Toilet soap will last much longer if a piece of thick silver paper is applied to one side of the new tablet. If the tablet is placed silver-paper side down in the soap dish waste will be avoided.

SOAP SAVING: Save all scraps of soap. When you have a fair quantity, roll in cloth, immerse in hot water for a few minutes and press into a solid ball.

SOAP (To cut): Fold a sheet of newspaper round the blade when cutting soap, and the knife will not stick.

Good Ideas

BABY'S APPLE: When baby first begins to eat an apple he usually drops it many times and it has to be washed or scraped or even thrown away. Core the apple, thread a length of white tape through the hole and hang it round baby's neck.

USE FOR OLD CLOCK: Have you got a clock which no longer goes? Don't throw it away. Keep it near your cooking stove, then when you put anything in the oven to bake get the time by your "good" clock and turn the hands of the old clock to that time—You can then go about your work without having to rely upon your memory as to the time you put the cake or other food into the oven.

YOU'LL FIND YOUR LATCH-KEY much more quickly in the dark if you thread it on to a length of white tape and sew this into a corner of your handbag.

WHEN THREADING BEADS if you dip your cotton in white of egg, then allow it to dry it will be as stiff as catgut, so that you can thread seed pearls or beads quite easily. The residue in an egg-shell after the egg has been used in cooking will do.

LACE FROM BELTS: Old discarded coloured belts can be made into gay-coloured laces if cut into ¼ inch strips. Also, punch some holes in a pair of gauntlet gloves and lace them up with improvised laces to match shoes.

A USE FOR CHRISTMAS CARDS: A wet day and children are bored—cut up Christmas cards in various-sized pieces. Award a small prize to child who puts together most successfully—result—a peaceful afternoon.

"ALARMING" NEWS: Alarm clock: Use your alarm clock to remind you of things. Put it on during the day so that it calls you to take a dish out of the oven; write a letter in time to catch the post, ring a friend or anything else you may forget.

USES FOR CAMPHOR

No home should be without a few pieces of camphor, as they have several uses. A cube kept in the same drawer as the silver keeps it from tarnishing, and one placed in a damp cupboard will keep it reasonably dry. It is a good idea to put a piece into new cushions when sewing them up. Not only does it keep moths away, but it gives a lovely odour to the cushion.

NIGHT-LIGHT: A small piece of camphor placed in a bowl of water so that it will float, may be lighted and will not only prove a good light, but also an excellent disinfectant.

OIL LAMP: If a camphor ball is put in the oil lamp; the oil will last longer and the lamp will give a brighter light.

USES FOR SALT

COMMON SALT: The variety of uses to which common salt can be put is endless. Here are a few not very generally known :–

Salt sprinkled over a carpet before sweeping will keep down dust, will help to brighten the colours in the pattern, and it is destructive to the eggs of moths.

KEEPS STOVES FREE FROM GREASE: Before frying, sprinkle the top of your stove or range with salt. The grease from the pan will not mark the stove, nor will there be any smell of burnt fat. The stove can be wiped over later with newspaper and will be quite free from grease.

IT KEEPS CUT FLOWERS fresh much longer if added to water every time it is changed.

REMOVES STAINS (Wine) from a tablecloth if used wet and left for one hour before washing in usual way.

PREVENTS MUSTARD from going sour if added when mixing.

REMOVES BURNT SUGAR FROM OVENS: When sugar or juice from pies runs over in the oven and scorches, sprinkle salt over the burning substance and it will check smoke and odour. Be liberal in the use of salt.

BURNED PIE-DISHES can be cleaned easily with a damp cloth dipped in salt.

CLEANS SPONGES: Sponges can be cleaned if soaked in strong salt water for 24 hours. Then rinse in cold water and lastly in warm water.

TO REMOVE THE MARKS OF BURNT FOOD: Mix egg shells with a little common salt.

PREVENTS MILK GOING SOUR: A pinch of salt added to milk will keep it from going sour.

TOOTHBRUSH (To make last longer): If a new toothbrush is soaked in water, to which a little salt has been added, it will last much longer.

PLATES STAINED THROUGH OVER-HEATING can be cleaned easily and quickly with a cork and salt: sprinkle salt over burnt part and rub with a slightly moistened cork.

CLEANS FIBRE: A tablespoonful of salt in a gallon of cold water is a good cleaning mixture to brush over your fibre mats.

WHEN WASHING STEPS IN FROSTY WEATHER add a tablespoonful of salt to the water. This will prevent ice forming.

USES FOR VINEGAR

PAINT BRUSHES: Paint brushes that have become

stiff will again become pliable if soaked bristle-deep in vinegar that is heated almost to the boiling point.

TO PREVENT DISCOLOURATION OF ALUMINIUM: Saucepans used for boiling eggs will not discolour if a few drops of vinegar are added to the water.

TO REMOVE RUST: Rusty articles, if soaked for two days in ordinary vinegar, taken out and wiped dry, will be found to be completely free from rust.

TO CLEAN GRATE: When cleaning grate or kitchen stove in wet weather mix the blacklead with vinegar instead of water. This will make the grate or stove much easier to clean and will give a brilliant and long-lasting shine.

GAS MANTLE (To make last): A new gas mantle soaked in vinegar for five minutes, dried, and then burnt off will last twice the usual time.

TO PREVENT PIPE CHOKING UP: A piece of soda and a little vinegar put in the sink and washed down with boiling water will take grease out of the pipe and save choking up.

CLEAN WINDOWS: When cleaning windows add a little vinegar to the water and it will make a nice clear polish.

TO REMOVE MORTAR AND PAINT FROM WINDOW GLASS: Mortar and paint can be easily removed from window glass with hot vinegar.

TO PREVENT LAMP SMOKING: If lamp smells or smokes put teaspoonful of vinegar in lamp. It will ensure a clear light and prevent unpleasant odour or smoke.

TO KEEP FISH FRESH: If fresh fish cannot be used at once, steep it in vinegar and it will keep for a few days.

TO SOFTEN SHOE POLISH: Shoe polish often becomes hard and dry; if this happens run a little vinegar over the top, put on lid and leave for a time before using.

USES FOR ASPIRIN

KEEP SOME ASPIRINS BY YOU: Doorsteps will not

freeze and become slippery in frosty weather if an aspirin tablet is crushed and dissolved in a cupful of warm water and is added to the washing water along with a tablespoonful of methylated spirits. An aspirin crushed to a powder and sprinkled in *the soles of the stockings* will be found of great benefit to those who suffer from chilblains.

ASPIRIN TABLETS WILL MAKE BRUSHES LIKE NEW if the brushes are immersed in water containing several tablets.

Economy Hints

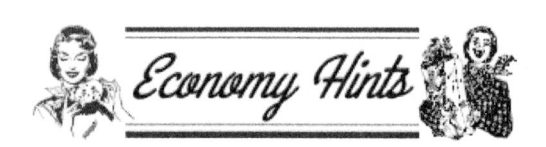

NEW DUSTBINS: New dustbins should be painted at the bottom inside and out. This will prevent rust and the dustbin will last much longer.

SAVE MATCHES: Split them from end to end with a sharp pen-knife, making sure that the inflammable part at the end is divided as well as the wood.

CURTAIN HINT: Turn your curtains upside down. You'll find a lot more wear in tops of them.

NEW CURTAINS: Never iron new curtains if it can be avoided as it helps to rot them. It is also a great saving (when pattern permits) to put a hem top and bottom and reverse them occasionally as this prevents one end being worn before the other.

TROUSERS: The bottoms of trousers will not get so worn if a small button is sewn where the trouser touches the instep of the shoe and another where it touches the heel; inside of course.

LAMP WICKS: A piece of frayed stocking web tacked to a short lamp wick enables the entire wick to be used.

EMERY PAPER: To lengthen the life of emery paper that has gone limp and creased, put it in a warm oven for five minutes.

RAZOR BLADES: The life of safety razor blades can

be lengthened consistently by either of the following methods: (1) Place the used blades or blade in a saucepan of cold water, bring to the boil and boil for five minutes; pour water off and dry carefully with a soft cloth; (2) Before using wipe edges carefully with a small piece of cloth dipped in ammonia. The blades will be found to be almost as sharp as ever.

PAPER BLINDS: In order to improve and double the life of paper blinds, get a piece of tape of medium width and paste it evenly down each edge. It prevents the torn edge so often seen and the blind will last twice as long.

SAVE ELECTRICITY: Wash your electric light bulbs regularly in soapy water: you don't get your full allowance of light from dirty bulbs.

PERSERVING CANDLES: Candles will burn at least half as long again if the following method is adopted: Hold the candle by the wick and give it a good coating of white varnish. Put away for two days to harden.

TORCH BATTERY when nearly exhausted will burn quite brightly again for just a short time if you heat it gently in front of the fire or put it in a warm oven.

ENVELOPES: It is a good idea to enclose an old envelope addressed to yourself when writing to anyone who corresponds with you regularly because it doesn't take a whole label to re-post it.

Stains

TO REMOVE STAINS FROM CARPETS: If the inkpot should accidently be upset on the carpet, do not try to soak it up with blotting paper, or mop it up with a wet towel, but instead, just pour a little cold water over it at once. The ink will float on the water, and when the carpet is rubbed dry no stain will show.

GREASE: Scrape off, cover with blotting or brown paper. Press the spot with a hot iron, taking care to keep the iron from touching the carpet. Brush up the pile while still hot. If a slight stain remains this can be removed with paste made from equal quantities of magnesia and Fuller's earth. Make the paste with boiling water and while still hot it should be spread thickly on the grease spots. When it has quite dried, brush off with a stiff broom. This process, too, may be repeated if a stain is particularly stubborn.

SCORCH: Rub with sour, heated milk and salt. Then shampoo.

SPLIT MILK: Wipe up and shampoo the affected area.

SOOT: Lift off gently by slipping stiff paper under it. Then sprinkle with dry salt and brush up. Shampoo the affected part.

BLACKLEAD: Leave till quite dry and then brush off and shampoo.

PARAFFIN: Apply a paste of Fuller's earth. When dry

wash off.

COAL TAR: Rub with paraffin then apply Fuller's earth.

PAINT: Rub with turpentine, then apply Fuller's earth.

VARNISH: Remove with methylated spirits.

IF THE NATURE OF THE STAIN IS UNKNOWN try warm water first, or apply a paste of bicarbonate of soda. When quite dry, brush off or remove with a vacuum.

MUD STAINS: Make a bowlful of strong soda water and rub the fabric along the weave with a rag dipped in this. This should remove any but the most obstinate stains, and these can be treated by brushing gently with cold tea, to which a pinch of cream tartar has been added.

MILDEW (To remove from kid gloves): Place them wrapped lightly in tissue paper in an airtight box containing a piece of rock ammonia. In a fortnight's time all traces of the spots will have disappeared.

RUST: Chop and boil a clean stalk of rhubarb in a cup of boiling water till reduced by half. Boil the stained portion in this solution for quarter-hour.

TAR: Sponge the stain with turpentine and rub well, unless the material is delicate. Wash in warm soapy water and rinse well.

MUDDY MACKINTOSH: Mere brushing will not remove mud stains from a mackintosh, so try rubbing the muddy place with a cut potato and then brushing again. All traces of mud can thus be removed.

SEA-WATER STAINS: To treat sea-water stains on a black handbag. Make a paste of blacklead and lemon-juice and cover the stain with it. Leave for an hour and then brush off with a stiff small brush.

To remove sea-water stains from *CANVAS SHOES* and *FLANNELS* apply a paste of Fuller's earth, brushing it off when dry. The stains can be removed from leather by the application of milk in which a little soda has been dissolved. Afterwards polish in the ordinary way.

MILDEW STAINS may be removed by rubbing with a

paste made by mixing two tablespoonfuls of water, one of powdered chalk and two of soap powder. The spots should afterwards be well rinsed and dried out of doors in the sunlight, which has a bleaching effect on them.

The easiest remedy for mildew on cloth is to dip the stained part in sour buttermilk and allows the article to bleach.

TO CLEAN LINEN BLINDS: Remove from window to a table. Scrub gently with a soft brush dipped in hot, soapy water, then wipe off suds with a soft cloth and roll up tightly. Return them to the windows then pull them down and allow to dry. If they are dark in colour it is sometimes possible to sponge them with warm water containing a little vinegar, but wipe them quickly with a dry cloth.

TO REMOVE FRUIT STAINS FROM HANDS moisten a crust of bread with vinegar and rub on the stains.

WINE STAINS: Dip the stained part in boiling milk and continue to boil until the mark disappears.

GRASS STAINS: Before putting away your cotton frocks for next year, remove the grass stains. Pour a little vinegar on to the stain over a plate, and work in. rinse off, then wash with soap and water.

INDELIBLE PENCIL MARKS may be removed from fabrics if soaked in alcohol and then washed. Lemon and dry salt will remove pencil marks on woodwork and paint.

TO REMOVE VERDIGRIS FROM BRASS: Clean with a soft brush dipped in liquid ammonia.

TEA STAINS: Soak the stained material in cold water, wash it, and then pour boiling water over the stain.

TO REMOVE IODINE STAINS from garments, moisten the surface with cold water and rub with bicarbonate of soda on both sides. It can then be washed in the ordinary way and all the stains should disappear.

INK STAINS may be removed from table linen, if

lemon juice, or milk is applied at once. When all the stains have been removed, steep the linen in cold water before washing it.

IRON MOULD: (1) To remove iron-mould from linen, wet the stained part and stretch over a jug of boiling water. Sprinkle with a few drops of oil or lemon, then allow to drip. Repeat the treatment and when the stain has gone wash the article as usual to get rid of the acid.

(2) Boil some rice and soak the stained material for four or five hours in the water.

TAR OR GREASE: When you get tar or grease or any fluid or the green from grass in your flannels, just rub it well over with the saliva of your mouth. You will find this an excellent hint.

EGG STAINS ON LINEN: When table linen is stained with egg it should be soaked in cold water before being laundered. Rub egg stains on china or silver with a rag dipped in cold water and kitchen salt. Be sure not to leave any salt on the silver.

SCORCH MARKS: (1) On white or fadeless materials can be removed if the threads are not actually burnt. Moisten the part with a drop or two of ammonia, wet with peroxide and dry out of doors.

(2) If when ironing, you happen to scorch anything, hold it under the tap and let cold water run through the scorched part. All traces of scorch marks will disappear at once.

Rub a half crown over that newly-made scorch mark, quick movements to and fro and it will disappear like magic (the mark, and not the half crown);

(3) Spread a paste made of starch and cold water over the stain, dry in the sun, then brush off.

BROWN LEATHER: Milk slightly warmed and mixed with a little washing soda will remove most stains from brown leather. Apply with a piece of flannel, beginning at the outside of each stain and working with a circular movement towards the centre.

STAINS ON FURNITURE

Heat marks will disappear from polished surfaces when rubbed with liquid metal polish and polished with a soft cloth and a little olive oil.

WHITE STAINS ON MAHOGANY: To remove these unsightly white stains caused by dishes being laid on a mahogany table the following treatment will be found effective: Apply a little spirit of camphor very lightly with a clean, soft rag—do not rub it in; then use a soft duster to polish. You will find that the stains can be instantly removed by this method.

AN IODINE STAIN on woodwork can be removed by spreading over it a paste of baking soda. When the soda dries, brush.

MOULD: To remove from furniture: Stir one teaspoonful of ammonia into half-a-pint of boiling water. Sponge off the mould. Wipe dry, then polish with furniture cream.

STAINED PIANO KEYS: Make a paste of whiting and methylated spirit, dab it on the keys and leave it for a time. Then rub over the keys with some more of the paste.

STAINED BRASS AND COPPER: Dipped in a little whiting, a piece of lemon rind will remove verdigris and clean old brass and copper.

BADLY STAINED MARBLE may be cleaned with a rag moistened with vinegar and dipped in salt; wash, dry and polish with furniture cream.

FOR RUST STAINS ON ANY TILE OR PORCELAIN: Mix a little vinegar with finely powdered pumice stone and the mixture will remove the stains.

YOUR BLUE-BAG will remove fly spots from mirrors; moisten it and rub the marks, then rinse away the blue.

CLEANER WITH IVY: To remove grease and shine from coats or suits take two or three handfuls of ivy leaves. Boil well, strain and bottle when cool—ready for

THE HOMECRAFT BOOK

use. Stains, etc., disappear when well rubbed with solution.

GREASY COAT-COLLAR: If the inside of a coat-collar becomes greasy and soiled, put a tablespoonful of ammonia into a pint of hot water, dip a clean nail-brush or old tooth-brush into this and brush the collar well. Dry by rubbing with a clean cloth, then hang in the open air for an hour or so.

REMOVING PAINT MARKS FROMWINDOW PANES: Splashes of paint can be removed from windows with a pencil or ink eraser, rubbing the marks lightly. If they prove obstinate use an old razor blade. (*See* Uses For Vinegar—page 55.)

FIREPLACE TILES: Those nasty smoke stains on the fireplace tiles will come off if you rub them briskly with a rag dipped in vinegar.

GLASS JUG OR DECANTER: Put tea leaves, water and teaspoon of vinegar into any glass decanter or jug that is stained and leave there over-night—they will remove all the blemishes (crushed egg-shells, water and vinegar will also do the same job).

BOTTLES—TO REMOVE STAINS: Add a little minced raw potato and vinegar. Shake well, the rinse in cold water. Or one tablespoonful tea leaves, one teaspoonful vinegar and warm water to fill. Stand for three or four hours, then shake, empty out and rinse.

TO REMOVE ODOURS: Half fill with cold water. Add a tablespoonful of dry mustard. Shake well. Stand for half an hour, then rinse with clear water.

ALUMINIUM STAINED: Apple peel or apple cores boiled for ten minutes in your aluminium teapot will remove tannin. Stains on aluminium saucepans can be removed the same way.

SOOT STAINS: To remove soot stains rub the spot with dry Indian meal or oatmeal.

TO CLEAN STAINED KNIVES: After using bath-brick on the knife-board, sprinkle on a little carbonate of soda and rub. It does not matter how stained or rusty knives may be, they will quickly be restored to their original surface.

INK STAINS ON SILVER INK STANDS can be removed with a mixture of whiting and sweet oil made into a thin paste and left on the stains for twenty-four hours before being washed off.

EGG STAINS ON CHINA OR SILVER can be removed by washing as usual and then rub with a damp cloth dipped in salt.

GREASE MARKS ON WALLPAPER can be treated with a paste of water and Fuller's earth. Mix to the consistency of a face pack and cover the stain liberally. Leave to dry completely before brushing off.

CARPET SOAP: Dissolve one packet of Lux in a little boiling water and allow to cool. To the jelly add four ounces of Fuller's earth. Mix well and keep in a jar for use on grease stains on carpets. Spirits of turpentine may be used if desired in this recipe, so as to work the mass into a paste which van be formed into balls. This carpet soap may be rubbed on grease stains on the finest wallpaper. It is also good for removing stains from the hands.

Getting Rid Of Pests

TO KEEP FLIES OFF WINDOWS and mirrors, sprinkle a little vinegar on the washing leather when cleaning them. This is especially effective during the summer months.

FERN AND FLIES: Nothing is more effective during summer-time than the common woodland fern for keeping house-flies at bay. Try a large one in a pot in the centre of the table.

ALL FRESH MEAT OR BACON let uncovered during the summer is a happy-hunting-ground for flies, especially the Green Fly. It lays its eggs there and after a few hours you find the meat covered with nests of white grubs. A good preventative: Sprinkle the meat generously with salt and pepper. Be sure to add the latter as salt on its own is not enough; the pepper added keeps the flies at bay.

WASPS: During hot weather, when wasps become a nuisance in the house half fill a saucer with water and add a teaspoonful of formalin (poured from the chemist) and a teaspoon of sugar. Stir well and place this out of reach of children and domestic animals. This mixture will attract the wasps and kill them off rapidly.

MOTHS: (1) Moths will not come near clothes sprinkled with turps;

(2) An excellent preventative for moths is to sponge

the inside of drawers and cupboards, where clothes are kept, with ammonia. Do the ledges the drawers rest on, too.

CLOVES (To keep away moths): Try shaking a few in wardrobes and in creases of couches and armchairs.

A QUICK WAY OF SUSPENDING MOTH BALLS in a cupboard or wardrobe if you haven't time to make legs, is to take a small tin and punch holes all around it. Make two holes in the lid to thread a loop of tape through, then put several moth balls inside the tin and hang it up.

PACK WINTER CLOTHES away in a trunk or in boxes and run broad adhesive tape round the edges to prevent moths from creeping in; if you seal the boxes properly you require neither moth balls nor newspaper. Cut your bars of household soap into small cakes and store among woollies until requires.

TO STORE BLANKETS: Powdered alum sprinkled over them is an excellent moth preventative.

IF MOTHS GET INTO CARPET lay a wet towel on the part affected and iron with a very hot iron until dry. This kills both moths and eggs.

BLACK BEETLES: A hot solution of one pound alum to three pints of boiling water poured down cracks and crevices will prevent black beetles from appearing up them;

(2) Strew powdered borax to exterminate beetles.

MICE: To get rid of mice, put a little oil of peppermint round the room.

A GOOD INSECTICIDE: Dump the contents of your cigarette ash trays into a large watering can full of water. When the liquid is deeply coloured and sprayed through the rose on garden plants it proves a good insecticide.

Seasonable Hints

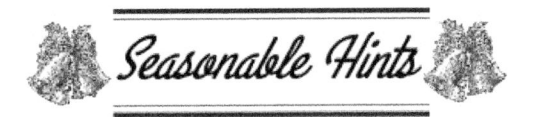

CHRISTMAS: At Christmas time our daily rules and regulations will naturally suffer many set-backs. Who cares? Christmas Week must always be a law unto itself; we would miss the worry and bustle, the frenzied shopping and the haphazard meals which are the things that make those few days the outstanding ones of the year. When Christmas has gone and everything else has been a huge success, we feel immensely pleased with ourselves; the knowledge that we have carried the household triumphantly through the fray leaves its own peculiar pleasant sensation of moral uplift and all's well.

We may, however, safeguard ourselves against too much strain by getting as many of the extras attended to as early as possible. Apart from this precaution we can solace conscience with the thought that the New Year is the recognized time for good resolutions—Christmas is Christmas.

CHRISTMAS EASE: If you want Christmas to run smoothly in the kitchen, you must plan your menus as far in advance as possible. Make a list of all the ingredients and quantities requires for dishes, table decorations, crackers, holly, crepe paper, serviettes and all the little etceteras that are needed to provide a good old Irish Christmas; then shop in good time.

When arranging your menus see that you provide only sufficient of the foods that don't keep well (such as green vegetables) for Christmas Day, and plan to serve tinned or root vegetables for the following days.

TO CUT dried fruit easily, use floured scissors. To prevent nuts and fruits from sinking into a cake, heat them before adding to cake batter.

CHRISTMAS CAKE: Cream together ½ lb. butter and ½ lb. castor sugar in a warm basin. Well whisk 3 eggs and add them gradually, alternatively with ¾ lb. flour, one teaspoonful of mixed spice, one teaspoonful of baking powder and a small pinch of salt (sifted), beating well after each addition: add ½ gill of brandy and ½ gill of warm milk by degrees. Then add 1 lb. currants, ¼ lb. sultanas, 2 ozs. Chopped raisins, ¼ lb. crystallised cherries (cut in halves), 2ozs. Shredded mixed peel, the grated rind of half a lemon or a few drops of lemon essence, 1 oz. of ground almonds, one ounce of chopped and blanched almonds. Mix all together thoroughly. Colour the mixture a pale brown with a little caramel. Bake in a moderate oven for about four hours. Your cake is cooked when it shrinks slightly away from the edges of the tin. If touched lightly with the finger it should spring back. Or, run a warmed skewer or knitting needle through the centre of cake; if it is cooked the steel should come out perfectly clean. Cool on a sieve. Leave for several days before icing.

ROYAL ICING FOR CHRISTMAS CAKE: 1 lb. of icing sugar, about 2 whites of eggs, 3 drops of acetic acid. Beat well until it is white, smooth and glossy; the more it is beaten the whiter it will become; a drop of ordinary washing blue will help to attain whiteness. While in use cover the bowl with a damp cloth to prevent it setting.

ALMOND ICING HINT: To make a little almond icing go a long way, mix with it some fine breadcrumbs. Not only is the consistency of the icing improved, but there is a noticeable difference in the taste.

TO KEEP CHRISTMAS CAKES: When rich fruit

cakes are quite cold, brush them over with a little brandy or rum; wrap them in greaseproof paper and keep them in a tin until 2 or 3 days before they are required when they must be taken out and iced. When the icing is hard the cake is ready.

OLD YULE TRIFLE: You will need: 1 sponge cake or jam roll, jam, custard, whipped cream, sherry, almonds.

Use a tall round sponge cake or jam roll. Cut into six pieces, spread two with raspberry jam and two with apricot jam. (If jam roll is used spread only two with apricot jam.) Put one slice of cake in dish, mix a few drops of brandy with 3 tablespoons sherry; pour a little of the wine on each until all cake and wine mixture are used up. Keep basting with what runs into dish until all the wine is absorbed by the sponge layers. Make custard (vanilla flavoured). When cold pour half over cake. Spike sides with split almonds. Leave the trifle until required then mask it all over with remainder of custard. Decorate with whipped cream.

This trifle will be an excellent stand-by around Christmas time. Remember, everyone doesn't appreciate Christmas Pudding.

MOST CHRISTMAS FARE IS SWEET OR LUSCIOUS and something crisp or savoury is often welcomed as a change, particularly by the menfolk, so try making some cheese airgrettes. If it is more convenient, they can be made the day before and heated in the oven when needed. Ingredients: 4ozs. flour, 1 oz. butter, 3 ozs parmesan cheese grated, 2 whole eggs and 1 yolk, ½ pint cold water, cayenne pepper, salt. Method: Put water and butter in a pan over fire, bring to the boil, add flour and stir over heat until the mixture leaves the side of the pan, cool; beat eggs in separately; add cheese. Drop into hot, deep fat, a tablespoonful at a time. Fry a golden brown. Serve sprinkled with grated cheese.

MINCE PIES: Mince pies are nice if the covers are stamped out first, and then the cuttings put together and rolled out for the linings. Butter pastry tins lightly, line with crust, put a good allowance of mincemeat in each, cover over, set in pans in a baking tin, and bake in a good oven—20 to 30 minutes. Sift sugar on them whilst hot.

IN SELECTING A TURKEY see that the legs are smooth and black, the spurs short, breast full and neck long. The feet should be supple.

2. Fowl with the feathers on last for a week, turkeys for a fortnight and geese not more than eight or nine days.

3. When baking, in order to derive full benefit from the supply of heating , be sure to latch your door securely. Do not open oven door unnecessarily.

ROAST GOOSE: This is an excellent way of cooking a goose and much more delicate than usual "stuffed-with-sage-and-onion" fashion. It is particularly good as a cold-supper dish, eaten with chutney. The goose should be trussed the day before it is wanted, and a lemon cut in halves left inside it. Remove, and pour boiling water through and over the bird. Steam for about 1 hour. Drain and dry with a napkin. Rub over with a little butter, flour and roast in a good oven till done and well browned.

TO USE UP GIBLETS: Make giblets into giblet broth with rice, parsley and thickened stock.

LEFT OVER TURKEY AND HAM: Mix small pieces of turkey and ham with dried celery and well flavoured mayonnaise and serve on a dish of lettuce for luncheon or supper.

Left over ham can be used in many dishes.
1. Add it to an omelette.
2. Mix it with a thick batter and cook like fritters.
3. Mix it with vegetables such as beans, peas or potatoes, salad.
4. Add as a flavouring to meat pies, rissoles, etc.
5. A nice supper dish can be made by cutting turkey and ham into small pieces and have ready a nice thick white sauce. Add turkey and ham to sauce while boiling, but do not boil, keep in warm position on stove until meat is heated thoroughly

through. Serve on hot buttered toast.

FOR THE YOUNG FOLKS: If you are throwing a Christmas Party for the children (and I know all of you who can afford it certainly will) here are a few hints that may help: Thin slices of pan, or any fancy loaf, buttered and sprinkled with "hundreds and thousands" are firm favourites. Chocolate biscuits, little jellies in small paper soufflé cases, potted meat sandwiches and above all don't forget the balloons.

HOLLY BERRIES are hard to save from birds. Here is one way of keeping them. When full red, cut off the best sprays with good long stems and plant these in a fairly deep box of earth. Keep in an airy place. These will be greatly prized for Christmas.

INEXPENSIVE CHRISTMAS PRESENTS: Very nice scarves can be made out of curtain net, cut into scarf length and threaded lengthwise only with wool on a bodkin, as if you were darning, leaving a piece of wool each end as a fringe. It's a good way of using up odd pieces of wool, making a jazz effect.

HINTS TO HOSTESSES: When it's a question of sweet or savoury, remember that your men guests will almost always vote for the savoury.

You may be fond of strong flavourings yourself, but remember that such things as onions or curry are sure to be an anathema to at least one of your guests.

Provide ash-trays and ash-trays and ash-trays all over the house, unless you want your homestead laid waste.

SUMMER

STAY-AT-HOME-HOLIDAY: Have a holiday, though you can't go away. Turn your house, if you have one! into a flat by shutting up—and forgetting—all rooms except the bedrooms in use and one living room, and get the family to do their own bedrooms. Nothing desperate will happen to the other rooms; they'll get dusty, but one good dust at the end of your holiday will put that right. Take picnic meals to the local park or common, "treat" yourself to an evening meal in a café. Forget the housework for a week; a little dust won't ruin your life, and you *need* a rest once a year.

AUTUMN

The things that are of Summer pass quickly away and henceforth we must attend mainly to active preparations for the late Autumn and Winter needs and comforts. While a chance still remains make the most of whatever fruit and vegetables are available in your garden or may be obtainable at reasonable prices in the shops. Save as much of them as you can by drying, pickling or preserving. All the processes are simple and fully explained in any good cookery book. A cupboard well stocked with bottled fruit and vegetables will be something to be thankful for in the coming winter.

Now is the time for a leisurely and systematic survey of your winter wardrobe, blanket chest, etc. Keep the likelihood of a fuel shortage in mind, and where possible make provision for little extras in warm clothing and furnishing. Don't allow a scrap of anything that will serve as fuel to go to waste. Try to keep adding to your fuel supplies anything that comes your way—turf, coal or timber—no matter how little it may be at a time. The time is getting short and keeping the home fires burning is going to be your big problem.

HOW TO KEEP WARM IN WINTER: Leave your jumper inside your skirt top during the day. Have your eiderdown under the top cover of your bed. If you can't procure hot water bottles get a couple of bricks. Heat them under any ordinary grate or on top of boiler, cover with a thin flannel and place in bed.

Washing and Ironing

WASHING

WASHING DAY: It is very questionable whether the housewife who works single-handed should keep up the old institution of a weekly washing day. After a day shared between the wash-tub and the mangle one's energies are overtaxed. It is far better to wash a few things at odd times; one can run through a handful of clothes without noticing it, and there is no need to keep dirty clothes about the house. Moreover, a small wash gets out the dirt without making one's hands rough and unpleasant.

WASHING DAY WISDOM: Shake all dusty things, like curtains, before soaking. Run your eye carefully over everything and mend where necessary. "A stitch in time" before washing will often save "nine" afterwards—especially if clothes are dried out-of-doors on a stormy day. Very grubby, articles and things stiffly starched, should have at least 24 hours' soaking. Better still, if they are put to soak on a Saturday night. All clothes, except woollens and coloured articles, should be steeped for twelve hours or longer. Don't, on any account, soak woollens. Handkerchiefs wash better if a handful of salt is added to the soaking water. Steep the articles according to the instructions on the packet of your favourite soap powder.

MULTI-COLOURED GARMENTS (To wash): When washing multi-coloured blouses, frocks, it is always safer to pour two or three drops of blue-black ink into the water. In some remarkable way this stops the colours from running. And always wash coloured things as quickly as possible—it's the hanging around in a damp state that causes colours to run more often than not.

TO WASH CORDUROY VELVETEEN steep the material in plenty of hot, soapy water, then lift it out and rinse in a bowl of clean, warm water. Do not wring at all, hang in the open to dry and if shaken frequently while drying, no pressing will be required.

CURTAINS: If a little turpentine is added to the water in which curtains are washed and a tablespoonful of the same is put into the starch they will iron up after being pulled well when wet, with the freshness and feeling of new ones.

OILY OVERALLS: Engineers' overalls and clothes that get stained with oil should be washed before they are used and starched with thin starch. This prevents the oil from soaking into the material. Then after use if they are put to soak in warm water containing a little ammonia, the grease will come out easily. The clothes should be starched each time they are washed, but the first starching is the most important.

TO BLEACH CLOTHES: To bleach clothes save the egg shells and on washing day put them in the boiler with the clothes; the lime in the shells is a splendid bleacher for white clothes.

To help whiten clothes and save soap, add a little pipeclay to the water in which the white clothes are boiled.

TO WHITEN CLOTHES: White clothes that have become yellow may be whitened by using cream of tartar—a teaspoon to a quart of water. Soak the clothes over-night in clean water to which the cream of tartar has been added and when ironed the clothes will be as white as snow.

WASHABLE RUGS: Soak in lukewarm, salted water for an hour or two, then wash in soap-suds to which a handful of borax has been added. A mechanical washing machine, would make quite light work of this job. Rinse till clear of all soap, pass through weak blue and hang in the shade to dry.

MAROCAIN AND CREPE FROCKS can be washed easily and don't shrink—they only appear to do so, and can be pulled out to their original shape when ironing. Remember to pull both ways under the iron.

TO PREVENT COLOURS RUNNING: 1. When washing pink or green linen or cotton fabrics, add vinegar to the rinsing water;

2. Violet or blue material should have a little borax added to the washing and rinsing water.

3. If afraid that colours will run in the wash soak the fabrics in water to which a tablespoonful of ox-gall has been added.

4. Never use too hot water for coloured clothes, and should they run, throw a handful of salt into a bowl of water with one tablespoonful of vinegar and immerse the fabrics in this immediately.

5. Salt added to rinsing water tends to prevent colours from running. It helps especially to fix black, blue and green. Vinegar used in the rinsing water helps to revive colours which have faded. The proportion to be used is one tablespoon to one quart of water.

PREVENT COLOURS FROM FADING OR RUNNING: A teaspoonful of Epsom salts in a gallon of water will prevent colours from fading or running in the wash.

HANDKERCHIEFS (To Wash White): If your handkerchiefs are not a good colour when washed, add a little hydrogen peroxide to the last rinsing water. It will remove fruit-stains and make the fabric snow-white. Do not use the peroxide extravagantly or it will rot the material.

MAKING TOWELS LAST: Always soak dirty towels over-night in cold water and a little borax to loosen the dirt; squeezing will clean them, scrubbing weakens the fibres. For the same reason wash towels more often, when they start to get soiled.

WASHING HOUSE SLIPPERS: To wash house slippers made of fabric soak in warm, soapy water to which you have added a little ammonia. Squeeze well till all dirt is expelled. Rinse in luke-warm water and squeeze gently in a thick towel , put on shoe trees and hang out of doors in a good wind to dry.

BLANKETS: This is by far the best way to wash blankets: Make a lather by dissolving two tablespoons of Lux and one teaspoonful of borax in a basin of lukewarm water, add this to half a bath of cold water; steep blankets in this for an hour or more. Then swish them backwards and forwards. Rinse in two or three cold waters, hang out dripping wet. By using this method, new blankets remain "new" almost indefinitely as natural oil is retained and even old blankets come up soft and fluffy

WOOLLENS

THE QUICKER YOU WASH WOOLLIES the better; very soiled woollies do better with two quick washes then one prolonged one, always using the same temperature of water for both washing and rinsing. To quicken drying, roll them up in a thick towel to squeeze out excess moisture before drying.

A LITTLE AMMONIA added to the water in which woollens are washed will improve them immensely. If a little is added to the water in which white clothes are soaked they will be much easier to wash.

BLACK STOCKINGS will not lose any of their colour in the wash if they're allowed to soak for several hours in warm water to which a little turpentine has been added.

CHILDREN'S BLACK WOOLLEN STOCKINGS or men's socks should be given a last rinse in strong blue water. This will help to keep them in a good colour and also seems to give them just a slight gloss.

TO KEEP SHAPE OF: (1) When the ribbing of your woollies stretches at the waist, sleeves and neck, the garments immediately lose their smart appearance. They will generally keep in shape, however, if you run a double thread around the edges of the ribbing before washing them;

(2) Woollies which have already lost their shape can often be made snug and neat again around the waist and neck: a spool of elastic thread should be procured and a few rows sewn around the back of the ribbing so as to draw it into shape again.

TO PREVENT FLUFF: Before washing your jumper, turn it inside out and this will prevent it going fluffy.

INSTEAD OF WRINGING dainty woollens after washing them, place each article between two clean towels and roll them out with a rolling-pin.

NEW CURTAINS: Add a handful of kitchen salt to the water when steeping new curtains. This removes the dressing and makes washing much easier.

HANDKERCHIEFS (To sterilize): (1) Add a small quantity of flowers of sulphur to the soap flakes in the boiler when laundering handkerchiefs. This will sterilize the hankies, which is especially necessary after colds. Rinse the handkerchiefs three or four times before handing them out; (2) Silk handkerchiefs and ribbons should be washed in salt and water and ironed wet to obtain the best results.

WASHING SILK FROCKS: Give a crisp new finish to your silk frocks when you wash them by adding a little methylated spirits to the rinsing water. Then spread the frock on a towel, roll up and leave for a few hours before ironing on wrong side with a fairly hot iron.

FEATHER PILLOWS which are soiled and leak feathers all over the place can be washed and re-made. Simply wash in their present covering, allow to dry thoroughly, then buy, or make, a new, strong ticking case.

Rub the inside of this well with beeswax to make it feather-proof. Leave a gap of 10 inches long in the new case, and cut one of the same length in the old, sew these gaps together. Shake the feathers from the old pillow into the new, remove the old cover by unpicking, and seam firmly.

FLANNEL (To prevent shrinking): When making flannel garments for children, soak the flannel first of all in cold water then wash it in the usual way. If you do this before making it up it will not shrink.

WHEN RIBBONS ARE WASHED wind them evenly around a bottle; then fill the bottle with very warm water and cork it. The ribbons will dry quickly.

FOR WASHING WHITE SILK and artificial silks a teaspoonful of methylated spirits in the rinsing water prevents the white from going yellow, and after ironing it imparts a gloss like new.

GUM (To rinse with): A few drops of gum added to the rinsing water, will give a delightful crispness to cotton dresses, lace and similar articles; it will also re-stiffen hats softened by rain.

OLD TIES can be washed and made up nearly as new. Before washing, tack the ties flat on each side, if time permits, the centre also, it's worth the trouble. Wash with Lux or Rinso and leave to dry for a while. Iron on the wrong side while still damp, taking out tacking thread before fully ironed to avoid creases.

GET INTO THE HABIT of giving your broom a weekly bath. Use hot soapsuds, then rinse, shake and hang in the open air.

Always wash new dishcloths and dusters before use; it takes out the dressing and makes them softer.

SPECTACLES (To prevent steaming up): If you wear spectacles when washing you may be troubled by the steam misting them. Rub the lenses with soap, then polish well and the glasses will keep clear.

LAUNDRY BASKET: Fix four castors to your laundry

basket and push it out to the drying line instead of lifting it (which wears you out) or dragging it (which wears it out).

BLUEING

TOO MUCH BLUE on your white things can be rectified if you soak them for a little while in a bowl of tepid water with three tablespoons of vinegar added.

CLOTHES STEEPED IN BLUE-WATER are often coloured in patches. If a spoonful of salt is put in the water, the blue will be distributed evenly.

STARCHING

WHEN MAKING a thick, clear starch, stir in a little cold water immediately after the boiling water has been mixed with the starch. This prevents a skin forming on the surface while it is becoming cool enough for use.

STARCH MADE WITH SOAPY WATER gives collars a beautiful gloss. It also prevents the iron from sticking.

TO MAKE COLD STARCH that will keep for several months, mix together one half pound of starch, one tablespoonful turpentine, one teaspoon powdered borax, three pints cold water.

AFTER USING STARCH place the bowl on one side and pour off the clear water. Then put the bowl in the oven for five minutes. The starch will cake and can be used another time.

TO AVOID STARCHING TABLECLOTHS: If half an ounce of methylated spirit be added to the last rinsing water, a tablecloth need not to be starched. If anything, it will look more glossy than usual.

WHEN MANGLING GARMENTS WITH BUTTONS, button up as when in use and place in the mangle with the buttons facing the top roller. Mangle slowly and there will be no broken buttons.

LOOK AFTER PRESS FASTENERS, always close them before putting through the mangle and they won't get flattened out.

TEA TOWELS: It is often found that tea towels leave a smear of fluff on the articles wiped by them. When this happens, dip the towel in a solution of weak starch water after washing.

DRYING CLOTHES

WINTER DRYING: A handful of common salt added to the rinsing water will prevent clothes from freezing on the line while drying in frosty weather.

WHEN DRYING SOCKS: Place a round of cardboard or stiff brown paper inside the ribbing to ensure quick drying.

INDOOR: If you have to dry clothes indoor, it's a good idea to put blouses and dresses on wooden coat hangers. They dry quickly in this way, and you can put more clothes on the line.

SMALL THINGS: Having to dry small things such as stockings in the house is often a problem. For drying stockings get an ordinary wooden coat hanger and 2 feet of wide white tape. Fold the tape into six loops and drawing-pin them to the hanger. A stocking is slipped through each loop and the hanger can be hooked over the window ledge or mantelpiece.

CHEATING SHOWERS: In rainy weather it is a good scheme to peg all very small white articles to a long strip of white cloth and peg the cloth to the line. Should rain come it is a matter of seconds to remove the strip of cloth and the articles with it.

WHEN TAKING CLOTHES OFF THE LINE walk along and remove alternate pegs first, then you won't have so many pegs to dispose of when actually gathering the clothes.

WHEN TAKING IN THE WASHING leave a pillow slip on the line till last, into which you put all the other articles.

IF BLANKETS ARE HARD AND FELTED after washing shake them vigorously, then hang on a line and beat them gently with a clean carpet-beater. The fluffiness will return and the appearance will be as new.

IRONING

COLD IRONING: I have found cold ironing a great fuel saver and use it for handkerchiefs, table mats, hand towels and such things. You lay the articles on a cold, hard surface, a marble slab for preference, and brush them evenly and firmly with a small, stiff-bristled brush, like a nailbrush, picking out points and corners just as you would with an iron. Brush again and leave until bone dry.

DAMPENING CLOTHES: (1) You will find this ironing hint very useful all the year round and especially in the warmer weather when some parts of an article get too dry and consequently the creases won't iron out; keep a small piece of damp sponge handy, and when you come to a dry crease just rub the sponge over it. By this method the material will be lightly and evenly dampened;

(2) When dampening clothes for ironing use hot water instead of cold; this penetrates more readily;

(3) Use an old pepper shaker filled with water for dampening down the clothes ready for ironing;

(4) When dampening your clothes for ironing, use a small bottle nearly filled with water and cut a small groove in one side of the cork.

SLEEVEBOARD: A small cricket bat makes a good sleeveboard for ironing. Cover the bat tightly with a piece of old blanket, then a piece of sheeting and sew in place;

(2) A folded newspaper makes an excellent sleeveboard; just fold it to size and insert it in the sleeve.

IRON (Stand for): Use a brick for standing your iron on, the iron will then retain the heat longer.

PLEATS (To keep in place): Use a hair grip to keep your pleats in place while pressing, etc.

IRON (Rusty): Rub a rusty iron with floor wax and salt to make it smooth.

PRESSING GARMENTS (To obtain a good finish): After

pressing as usual with a damp cloth, iron immediately with a dry cloth; This keeps the steam in and gives a beautiful finish.

IRON TONICS: When you have had a large wash, place towels, sheets, pillow cases and other flat things underneath the ironing sheet while the rest of the clothes are being ironed. The articles underneath the sheet will then need practically no more ironing.

MEN'S TROUSERS (To press): When pressing men's trousers use a damp cloth and hot iron. Always start work at the knee where bagginess occurs, spread the damp cloth over the knee then press the place firmly, first left then right, till the whole knee area has been ironed. This will shrink the bagginess back into shape.

PADDED SHOULDERS: When pressing a coat or jacket with padded shoulders, fit a small bowl into the shoulders, out your hand into the bowl and place a damp cloth over the shoulder pad. This makes the job much easier.

IRON STICKING (To prevent): A teaspoonful of salt in a pint of boiled starch gives a brilliant gloss and prevents the iron from sticking.

IRONING (Foot relief while): On ironing day try standing on a soft, thick rug and note if it will prevent the feet becoming tired as they would otherwise be.

The Needlewoman

HOUSEWIFE'S APRON: An apron with pockets in which she can carry some of her working equipment is no end of a boon to a busy housewife. Instead of having to waste time fetching the small things she needs for her work, she has them ready to hand in one of the apron pockets.

Make garments from a strong and durable material. See that it is wide enough to wrap well round the waist towards the back. Machine on to it about six strong pockets. The two upper pockets should be wide and deep enough to hold a good supply of pegs on wash-day. A lower row of four smaller pockets will carry work-gloves, polishing cloth, polish, or a notebook and a pencil. One of the smaller pockets should be lined with mackintosh or thin rubber, so that soap or a damp cloth could be slipped into it. Bind pockets and apron edges with a strong cotton banding in a contrasting colour.

HANDY MORNING APRONS can be made from the skirt of old frocks. Cut up the seams, hem and stitch on the ties for the waist.

WORN TOWELS (Uses for): When rough or worn towels are beyond further use for their original purpose, do not use them for dusters or rubbers; they leave behind them a most irritating fluff. A much better idea is to quilt together two or three layers for use as a bath-mat. The mat may be cut in a round, oblong or square shape, and the edges bound with bright-coloured tape. You may then, if you wish, work a large flower in wool on the corner, or trace the words "Bath Mat" in large chain stitch.

WORN TURKISH TOWELS can be made into children's feeders, bath gloves, lavatory cloths and babies' squares.

WORN BLANKETS (Uses for): Make a quiltette from the best parts of very old and worn blankets by cutting out squares of the blanket and herring-boning them together. With a wire brush teasel the blanket material to make it very soft and fluffy. Make a cover from old curtains, material or patchwork. Machine-stitch diagonally.

A WORN BED-SHEET especially a linen one, worn too thin for bed use. Cut it up the centre, hem raw edges, buy a few yards inch lace, sew it on the full lengths then dye lot any shade desired, you have a pair of window curtains, which will give good wear.

OLD STOCKINGS (Uses for): If you have many old stockings which are useless for wear, why not make a stocking rug out of them? Here's how you make it: cut the stockings round and round slightly on the cross, about ½ inch to ¾ inch wide into a ball. The strip is then threaded through a hooked rug needle and used on sacking exactly as if it were rug wool. A little more care must be taken to see that the loop does not slip than in using wool, but the result is well worth the trouble.

WHEN STOCKINGS ARE PAST WEARING and repairing if they are cut round and round spirally, about ¾ ins. wide, this strip which curls into a long tube is excellent for crocheting with a bone hook into blankets for the baby's cot, or tea cosy or slipper tops.

SOCKLETS (To make): Socklets will save your stockings, keep your feet warm and save darning. You can make them out of machine-knitted jumpers, too old for wear. Use an old pair of socks or stockings as a pattern. Sew with tight button-hole-stitch.

PILLOW CASES (Worn): Pillow cases that have become worn in the centre need not be discarded. Take a large white handkerchief and stitch it in the centre of the pillow case with the corners pointing to the top and bottom, giving a diamond effect. Then, if you like, stitch a small lace medallion in the centre or embroider your monogram there.

USE FOR WORN NIGHTDRESS: It is generally the upper part of a nightdress that wears out first, while the lower part remains perfectly whole. If the shabby piece is cut off and a hem made with a tape running through, this will make an excellent bag for protecting an evening frock.

WORN TABLE LINEN can be mended neatly and quickly by tacking a piece of fine muslin behind the thin part and then darning with the sewing machine.

LINEN (To prolong life of): When the hem-stitched edges of pillow cases and sheets tear away, stitch rick-rack braid over the hem-stitching.

GLOVE TIP: When openwork summer gloves wear in holes at finger tips and they are beyond repair do not throw them away, but cut about 1½ ins. to 2 ins. off the top of each finger and thumb. Pull gloves inside-out and turn cut edges over about ¼ inch and fasten down neatly. Turn back on right side and you have an attractive pair of mittens to wear.

GLOVES (To mend): A good way to mend a chamois leather or kid glove is to turn the glove inside-out, draw the edges of the tear closely together and press a piece of adhesive tape carefully over the damaged part; be sure the edges of the tape are properly stuck and you should have an invisible repair.

WHEN DARNING GLOVES (1) a clothes peg thrust into a finger will act as the necessary support.

(2) To darn the fingers of gloves drop a marble into the

finger that needs darning. This holds it out straight and one can get at the darn so much more easily and a much neater piece of work is the result.

CHAMOIS LEATHER GLOVES: Always wash chamois leather gloves before you mend them: using a fine needle, mend while they are still wet.

COTTON FROCKS (To mend): If you get a tear on a cotton or silk frock you can mend it invisibly by placing the frock or other article wrong-side-up on a table, put the torn edges neatly together and have a piece of the same material, enough to cover the tear, brush with white of egg and out it in place on the frock; it will stick on the material. Press with a hot iron, and it neatly done the right side will be perfect, with no sign of a break; and what is more, it can be washed.

SCHOOL-GIRLS' BLOUSES (To mend): School-girls' blouses and pyjama-coats usually "go" under the arms first, put an extra half-lining here from scraps of material when making them to provide a basis for easy mending.

A BUTTON TIP: When a button has to stand hard usage; sew it on across a darning needle placed between it and the cloth. When the sewing is finished, pull out the darning needle and the button will be sufficiently loose to stand jerks and strains without being torn off.

SETS OF BUTTONS: When you cut a set of fancy buttons off a blouse, coat, skirt, etc., thread each set on a piece of coloured silk. It is much handier to have them together this way than to hunt through the button box when you need them.

ANCHORAGE FOR BUTTONS: A sudden tug often brings away button and bit of material too. This is less likely to happen if you "back" each button with a small circle of material on the wrong side of the garment, and sew well through.

MATCHING BUTTONS: Easy way to make matching buttons for your jumper: Pierce a hole in the centre of an ordinary linen button, then sewing from hole to the edge of the button over and over, cover a set of buttons with left-over wool from your jumper.

A BUTTON BOX: Keep a button box and drop into it all odd buttons cut from old garments; hooks and eyes and press-studs, too.

DUSTERS: Do not discard your thin and worn dusters. Place two together, machine round the edges and across the holes and you will then have one almost as good as new. Make dusters by joining together old stocking-tops.

PATENT FASTENERS: When sewing on patent fasteners, first sew on all required on one side of skirt, opening etc. Rub chalk or talcum powder on fasteners, press on other side of opening and you will have a clear impression of the absolutely correct position in which to sew the corresponding halves of fasteners.

WHEN KNITTED THINGS ARE "HOPELESS": When small boys (or older people) wear their woven garments into holes or wear them too thin to be mended, there is no need to relegate them even to the rag bag. They must be converted into excellent "additional" bedding or will come in for underlays to protect better mattresses.

They should first be thoroughly well washed and ironed whilst still damp, to make them as flat as possible. The pieces are then machined together and slipped into a cover of cretonne or print. All kinds of woolen garments, including the legs and tops of men's woolen socks, may be used up in this way.

NEW AND ATTRACTIVE SUN-BATHING SUITS FOR CHILDREN can be made by knitting up old balls of wool. The various colours give a pretty effect.

BOY'S JACKET WORN AT ELBOWS: If a boy's jacket is badly worn at elbows, patches from worn-out pair of leather gloves will save the day. The patches should be in the form of a semi-circle sewn in with a straight line to the other sleeve seam and the rounded edge stitched down towards the inside of the elbow.

BOYS' TROUSERS (Worn seats of): Boys have such a terrible way of wearing out seats of their trousers before the rest of the garment is outworn that some way of preventing this is imperative.

A very good plan is to seize the moment when the first sign of going threadbare appears. A patch of the same material should be set in directly under the coming hole. Stitch it on the right side using thread that matches exactly. Now machine across and across in vertical rows, as closely together as possible.

Take particular care to stitch down any frayed edges.

WOOLLENS (To repair): If you have hard-working males who wear holes in their underwear beneath the arms in no time at all take something white wool and knit square patches the required size; these are neat, soft and stretchy and do not pull fresh holes in the garment. In a house where the kiddies are just learning to knit, these patches would be an excellent thing to start them on.

TO DARN STOCKINGS: (1) Stockings are precious now; if you have to darn them try this way: get scraps of net from worn-out undies and lay them over the holes or tin parts and darn down neatly into position. (2) There is no need to spend your money on darning silks, cut top off an old stocking of a matching shade and use the unraveled silk to mend your laddered hose.

WORN STIFF COLLARS: Worn starched collars make good shoulder pads for dresses and coats.

WORN SHIRT (To make use of): From a man's discarded shirt enough sound material can be salvaged to make a school blouse for a small girl.

WORN FLANNEL TROUSERS: Father's old flannel trousers provide material for a warm little frock. Use the top part from the bodice and make a gored skirt from the leg portions. Trim with contrasting collar and cuffs.

CHILD'S JUMPER (To enlarge): To enlarge child's jumper without unpicking it merely undo the sides and sleeve seams and insert a contrasting crocheted strip along between the two edges.

WHEN MAKING A NEW FROCK buy some extra material and make an apron to wear with it. It won't be so noticeable and will do for repairs later on when dress needs it.

CUTTING FLIMSY MATERIAL. When cutting flimsy material, dip scissors in boiling water and you'll have no trouble.

A FALSE FRONT OR TWO TO WEAR under your costume coat rings the changes smartly. The false front may be a mere strip of striped material with a bow at the neck, and the lower edge tucked into the skirt, or a waistcoat front with trim collar and points passed under the belt of the skirt.

SHOULDER PADS (Filling for): When making shoulder pads for coats or dresses, instead of filling them with cotton wool, use dried lavender. The scent will keep moths away and prevent your dress and coat getting that tired, stale smell which thick things acquire so easily in the winter.

COLOURED THREAD: When dyeing articles of clothing, etc., run a few lengths of white thread through the article before dipping. You will then have the right colour thread for alternatives.

THREAD RUNS EASILY: When next you have to sew buttons on thick material, such as an overcoat, you will find it helps if you draw some strong thread through soap for this purpose. This preliminary will strengthen the thread and also make it slip easily though the fabric.

WHEN THREADING A MACHINE NEEDLE hold a piece of white paper beneath the needle and see how quickly the thread goes through.

COTTON KNOTTING (To prevent): To prevent cotton knotting, thread through your needle before cutting off from the reel.

DARNING WOOL: After darning from a new card of wool, always nick the top of the card with a scissors and slip the end of the wool in. This avoids looking for the end, which is very annoying with dark wool.

NEEDLES (To keep from rust): Pins and needles, etc., are kept bright and free from rust if sheep's wool is used for stuffing cases or pin cushions as a quantity of oil present in the wool prevents the steel rusting.

KNITTING NEEDLES BENT: If your bone knitting needles are bent, steep them in very hot water and straighten; plunge them into cold water to keep their shape.

THREAD AND TAPE ECONOMY: Pull out tacking threads without cutting and wind them round on empty reel for use again and again. Always measure the exact length of tape binding or ribbon or sew it on before cutting, never cut first by guess work and waste a couple of inches.

ELASTIC ECONOMY: Sew tape to each end of elastic for threading in underwear and tie. It can be removed before washing and will last much longer, especially for children's use.

TO SHARPEN SCISSORS: After working the open blades of scissors on each side of a narrow-neck bottle you will find a blunt scissors will cut quite well.

WHEN LETTING DOWN HEMS of coat, frock or skirt, take piece of damp soap and rub it along the old hem mark on the wrong side; press in the usual way with damp cloth. The old mark will disappear and articles look quite new again.

Beauty

YOUR COMPLEXION

DRY SKIN: A skin which feels taut after washing and which is rough, cracked or scurfy is caused by under-activity of fat glands due to wrong diet, careless treatment, or a health condition such as thyroid deficiency, etc. Cure: Take as much milk, fruit, vegetables, salads and fats as possible, and drink more water between meals. Avoid hot water, harsh soap, astringents, liquid foundations, vanishing creams and all but the mildest face packs. Use an easily absorbed skin food both for nourishing and protecting the skin. Cream the face before and after soap-and-water wash and, if possible, have all-over oil rubs and oil face masks. Don't stir over hot fires or near hot-water pipes and protect the skin with cream when sitting under an electric hair-dryer or when cooking or washing clothes.

UNDER-NOURISHED SKIN: This type of skin is usually dry and laky. The best treatment for it is to administer an egg and oil mask once a week; to use a thin film of skin food in preference to vanishing cream as a foundation for powder, and to leave a thin film on at night. Massage every day with a good oily skin food. Be careful of your choice of toilet soap if you use soap on your face.

GREASY SKIN: A greasy sin is a skin that is not acting properly. Lather and scrub your complexion, using a soft brush and keep on until the face tingles, rinse in clean water and dry, then pat into face some astringent lotion. Powdered oatmeal added to the face powder: 1 part oatmeal to 3 parts powder helps to absorb the grease and keep the sin matt and free from shine. "Astringent Lotion": Elder-flower water, 3 oz.; witch-hazel extract, 3 ozs.; gin 1 oz.; distilled water, 6 ozs.

SOAPS: The woman with a fire, delicate skin should be very careful in the choice of her toilet soap. Only a really good super-fatted one should be used, and it should never be applied to the face with cold water. Use lukewarm water and make a lather of soap in the hands, using them instead of a face glove or wash cloth. All traces of soap should be carefully washed off with clear water. If a dash of cold water is given to the face and throat after the soap suds have been removed, the skin will look and feel much fresher.

SKIN CLEANSING: Correct skin cleansing is of vital importance. Cleanse your face and neck at bedtime with cream. Follow this with a soap and water wash, using a bland soap and, if possible, rain water or water to which you have added a teaspoonful of fine oatmeal. In the morning splash the face with cold water, or if your skin is dry cleanse with complexion milk.

ENLARGED PORES: In a greasy skin the pores often become enlarged, especially on and around the nose. This condition can be prevented or alleviated by washing the face in soft, tepid—never hot—water, by the use of astringent lotions such as witch hazel and, in serious cases, by applications of face packs once or twice a week.

BLACKHEADS: Gentle friction with a rubber sponge will help to remove blackheads. Apply the following lotion at bedtime: Powdered sulphur, 1dram; zinc oxide, 3 drams;

calamine, 3 drams; glycerine, 2 drams; water, 4 ozs.

SPOTTY COMPLEXION: Spots and blackheads often make their appearance on the skin in the spring. In addition to a lighter diet, eat raw carrots chopped up in salads, raw, red cabbage, finely shredded, cooked beet and all vegetables containing iron. Drink liquid in which raisins have been steeped over-night—it's a magical blood purifier.

TIRED SKIN: Try one or two face packs—the kind ready prepared and sold in tubes, if obtainable. If not, a skin-brisking treatment twice a week for a fortnight. This means, first, massage with any cold cream or skin food. Next, a thorough wash with hot water and plenty of soap, lastly rinsing in several lots of cold water. Dry skins need a little extra skin food on the night of the treatment.

LINES: Worry line round the mouth make the loveliest face look weary. Place the fingers on the chin and work them up and round the outer corners of the mouth, in towards the nostrils, and out again to the cheeks. Apply an anti-wrinkle cream at bedtime.

REJUVENATE YOUR FACE: Going out for an evening and you're dead to the world? Cleanse your face, make a cotton wool mask, soak it with skin tonic and place it in position, pressing it on the face with the finger-tips. Relax under it for ten minutes. Remove and make up your rejuvenated face.

FRECKLE CURE: Mix one teaspoonful of flowers of sulphur into a paste with some new milk. Cover the face with a thin layer on going to bed and allow to dry on. Wash it off next morning with warm water. This cures freckles, when in their early stages.

TO REMOVE FRECKLES: Mix together equal parts of peroxide of hydrogen (10 vol.), strained lemon juice, rosewater and glycerine. With a fine camel-hair brush apply the mixture, painting it on each individual freckle. It should be allowed to dry on the skin. This mixture ought to be prepared in small quantities, for the first two ingredients lose their strength through exposure to light and air. Bathing the skin in buttermilk when it can be obtained fresh (it is useless otherwise) is an excellent remedy for freckles and sunburn.

LEMON JUICE (A good astringent): As an astringent, lemon juice is hard to beat. If you suffer from enlarged pores, dab a little on the skin night and morning; a wonderful difference will soon be noticed.

POTATO BLEACH: The juice from a potato makes an excellent bleach for whitening the skin. Wash a large potato, cut it in slices, about ½ inch thick, and rub over the face, neck and hands. Do it at night after thoroughly cleaning the skin and allow the juice to remain on till next morning. Wash off with lukewarm water without soap.

SALT AND BEAUTY: Slat water, when sea-bathing, should not be allowed to dry on the face and throat. It causes wrinkles and a coarse skin. A little fresh water or rosewater should be taken to the beach in a small bottle and with a pad of cotton wool the sea salt washed from the face after coming out of the water. Salt baths are very beneficial for tired nerves and also for relieving foot troubles, but when taking such a bath the water should not be used for the face. The many wrinkles seen on the faces of old fishermen have generally been attributed to the salt water and the salted air in which they spend their lives. Too much salt, when taken as a condiment is said to induce a coarse, wrinkled skin.

HONEY FOR BEAUTY: Honey is quite invaluable as a toilet article. If a small jar is kept in the bathroom or on the dressing-table it will be useful for rubbing into rough, chapped hands during wintry weather and for chapped lips. It helps to soften and whiten the skin and when mixed with half its quantity of rose or orange flower water, makes the hands very soft and white. It should be rubbed into the skin when they are half dry and the drying finished with a soft towel.

YOUR LIPS

LOVELY LIPS: To keep the lips youthful and the skin round the mouth unlined, try not to tense the mouth continually. Always keep the lips very slightly parted—and this will do so much towards preserving that soft and youthful look. And here's a little exercise to do every evening. After you've creamed your face, say the alphabet through very, very quickly "mouthing" each letter quite distinctly.

FOR THOSE PAINFUL AND UNSIGHTLY BLISTERS (commonly called cold sores) which form on the lips and about the mouth apply spirits of camphor; this may sting for a few seconds, but it dries up the blister better than anything else. You should never put grease on these little sores until they are healed. Afterwards if any red mark if left, apply a little camphor ice each night. If your lips are apt to crack in winter, rub a little warmed olive oil or some camphor ice into them.

YOUR EYES

TIRED EYES (1) will be refreshed after bathing with a solution of one part vinegar to two parts water.

MAKE THEM SPARKLE by bathing them twice a day in tepid water containing boric crystals (¼ teaspoonful to 1 pint water) or use a proper eye lotion.

TIRED EYES: (2) If the eyes feel dull and tired, wring out a pocket handkerchief in lukewarm water, fold it like a bandage and sprinkle two or three drops of eau-de-Cologne on it, lay it lightly across the eyes, and rest in a darkened room for about ten minutes. This will refresh and help to brighten the eyes, and it an excellent treatment for improving the eyes before going to a dance or other entertainment.

TO PREVENT STRAIN: Before you tackle that sewing basket make a good resolution. Every time you sew on a button or finish darning a sock screw up your eyes, relax them and blink half-a-dozen times. Finally, roll them in circular movements. This will keep your eyes bright and prevent any risk of strain.

EYELASHES (To grow): Eyelashes grow very slowly but they can be coaxed to develop into the loveliest fringe. Coconut oil, white Vaseline, a mixture of olive oil with a few drops of castor oil or lanoline can be used to encourage them to grow. Use a tiny eyelash brush and brush whichever preparation you choose well into the roots, being careful not to get it inside the lid. (None of these oils will do any harm, but anything inside the lid or on the eyeball will cause discomfort and smarting).

TREATMENT OF WRINKLES AND LINES AROUND THE EYES: Daily massage with almond or olive oil which has been slightly warmed is the best thing. Place a small quantity of oil in a cup and dip the second finger of each hand in the oil and, starting on the upper lids and at the inner corners of the eye, pat in the oil with slow gentle dabs. Take care not to drag the fingers along the skin as this tends to stretch it. Work to the outer corners of the eyes, then back along the lower lids to the nose. In the morning remove all greasiness with a pad of cotton wool dipped in witch hazel.

YOUR NOSE

IF YOUR NOSE IS RED indigestion is frequently the cause unless exposure to cold weather is to blame. If indigestion is suspected, try to take more exercise to stimulate the circulation and look carefully into the matter of your diet. Use a slightly darker face powder to tone down the colour of your nose. If cold winds make your nose red apply cream and powder before going out-of-doors or a good powder cream. Do not go too near the fire when you come in.

YOUR TEETH

TO WHITEN THE TEETH: Peroxide of hydrogen, 1 part to seven parts water, may be used occasionally to brush the teeth when they have a tendency to become yellow and dull, but it should not be used every day.

TO REMOVE STAINS: A little cigar or cigarette ash mixed with toothpaste will remove stains from teeth and will whiten discoloured teeth.

YOUR JAWS

JAW LINE: If yours is heavy or sagging, firm patting movements with the palm of the hand, upwards towards the ears should be carried out each day, using an astringent lotion.

YOUR CHEEKS

HOLLOW CHEEKS: Hollow cheeks which have lost their attractive roundness, may be your problem. Then do this exercise once or twice each day. Move the head as far back as it will go and look up, opening the eyes to their fullest extent. Fill the cheeks with air and blow it out slowly in a series of small puffs.

YOUR HAIR

TAKING CARE OF YOUR HAIR: Once a month but 1 oz. of olive oil and when you have thoroughly brushed and combed your hair, heat the olive oil and massage it well into the scalp. Finish off the treatment by shampooing in the ordinary way, finally rinsing with lemon juice. (1 tablespoonful of lemon juice to 1 pint water). You will be delighted with the beautiful gloss your hair will have after this treatment.

FAIR HAIR (To brighten): Fair hair that is losing its

bright tints can be given golden lights by rinsing in chamomile lotion. First thoroughly shampoo the hair and rinse it in two separate waters. Put 2 ounces of camomile flowers in a large jug, pour over them a pint of boiling water and stir. Cover the jug and allow to stand for 15 minutes. Strain off and use as a last rinse for the hair, pouring the liquid over the head again and again, dry with a warm towel and follow with a good brushing, smearing the brush with a few drops of golden brilliantine.

WHITE HAIR (To bleach): Get rid of that yellowish look and give yourself a perfect head of silver hair by using the juice of a lemon or a little washing blue in the shampoo rinse, allowing the locks to soak well in this solution.

HAIR BEAUTY IN WARM WEATHER: Give the hair plenty of combing and an air bath whenever possible. Exposure to the rays of the sun during the hottest hours of the day is not good for the hair, but ventilation will improve the colour, making it brighter and glossier and help to increase the growth.

GETTING RID OF DANDRUFF: Dandruff brings nearly every known hair trouble in its train. Dry hair gets brittle and lifeless, greasy scalps become clogged and inactive and grey hairs soon make their appearance if dandruff is neglected. Remember that dandruff is not dirt but is caused by a germ and is very infectious. Using another person's brush or comb, or trying on someone else's hat can quite easily pass on the trouble. The treatment consists in using special ointment and an antiseptic shampoo. An ointment which is both effective and inexpensive is composed of lanoline, 1 oz; precipitated sulphur, 60 grams. You massage a little of the ointment into the scalp for three successive nights. On the fourth night the hair should be shampooed with a coal-tar shampoo. Repeat the treatment every twelve days until every trace of dandruff has disappeared.

SHAMPOO (To choose): Fair hair: Camomile Shampoo;

Reddish hair: Henna or Camomile; Brown Hair: Tar Shampoo; Blue-Black hair: Egg Shampoo (made by adding a beaten yolk of egg to ordinary shampoo when ready).

TO SET: An excellent setting lotion can be made by taking the white of an egg and adding 4 times the amount of water. Comb the mixture through the hair. It makes a perfect setting lotion and gives a lovely gloss to the hair.

TO PERFUME: To perfume the hair, sew a tiny sachet perfumed with your favourite scent into the lining of your hat, another in the centre of your hair net. This is better than spraying perfume on the hair, which often tends to encourage greyness.

DO YOU SMOKE? Be moderate or your health and skin will suffer. Shampoo your hair twice as often as your non-smoking friend, and air your clothes in a draught, for stale smoke clings to the hair and fabrics. Use a holder to keep the upper lip and fingers free from discolouration and a refreshing mouth-wash night and morning.

VINEGAR INDISPENSABLE IN YOUR TOILET CUPBOARD: For brunettes with greasy hair it can be mixed with water and applied to the hair direct, then rinsed off with rain-water. It keeps the colour and makes it scrupulously clean and silky. (Lemon juice for blondes).

PREMATURELY GREY HAIR: Hair usually retains its colour until the forties, signs of greyness before then may be termed premature and can often be arrested. *CAUSE*: Congestion of the scalp and feeble head circulation. Constant headaches, anaemia, nerve shock or exhaustion. Severe illness or rheumatic tendency, or excessive drying of the hair by cheap permanent waving. *CURE*: Take plenty of iron-rich foods—oatmeal, liver, prunes, figs, all dark-green vegetables, particularly watercress, broccoli, turnip tops and plenty of vitamin B. foods, such as wholemeal yeast and all-bran. Have a course of neck and scalp massage, professional if possible, and increase the time spent on hair brushing and fingertip massage. Correct dryness with oily-type tonics.

YOUR SHOULDERS

TO WHITEN SHOULDERS FOR AN EVENING: To whiten shoulders temporarily, bathe with warm milk, sprinkle thickly with fine oatmeal, and rub the oatmeal into the skin until it is quite dry. Then add the usual complexion powder.

YOUR ARMS

RED, PIMPLY ARMS respond to a special goose-flesh paste. Make a paste of a little fine oatmeal, powdered pumice and cold cream, thinned out with a little peroxide. Massage the mixture into the skin with firm strokes and, after bathing, rub in a hand lotion or soothing jelly.

THE TOO-PLUMP ARM: To reduce the too-plump arm, massage every night and morning with a mixture of one part spirits of camphor and three parts orange-flower water. First bathe the arms, then massage, using the lotion in place of a cream and working from the wrists towards the elbows and from the elbows towards the shoulders.

ELBOWS AND ARMS: So often, short-sleeved summer frocks reveal arms that are backed with round, goose-pimply flesh and hard, sandpaper elbows. The cause of both is excessive dryness and the treatment is the same for both: Every night, rub in a little of whatever nourishing preparation you have, oil, skin food or cold cream. When you wash, lather a stiff nail brush with a good face soap and scrub at the spots or roughness.

Dry briskly and always apply more cream after the wash to counteract the drying effect of the water.

YOUR HANDS

CARE OF YOUR HANDS: Before starting work, rub a little non-greasy cream into your hands. This will prevent dust and dirt penetrating the pores and will keep your hands soft and white. If your hands have been neglected, here is a cream you can make yourself to soften and whiten them: You need 1 oz. of zinc ointment and Lanoline, add the oil and beat together. Massaged in last thing at night this is an excellent remedy for dry and wrinkled hands. If you have to wash your hands many times a day, be sure to rinse them in cold water after washing them in warm; this will close the pores and the hands will keep clean much longer.

SPRING CLEAN YOUR HANDS: Nicotine stains on fingers will usually yield to treatment with hydrogen peroxide, and ink will come off after rubbing with soapy pumice stone. Callouses need the pumice too, and plenty of nourishment to counteract the drying.

TO REMOVE STAINS FROM HANDS: To remove stains from the hands after housework or cooking, rub over with a mixture of vinegar and water, equal parts, or a piece of toilet pumice stone smeared with soap.

SAVE YOUR HANDS: Before you throw away old gloves, snip out the fingers and thumb, slip one of them on your thumb before you peel potatoes or onions and your hands won't be so rough and grimed after the operation. Naturally, this hint saves any possible "thumb cuts" too.

ENLARGED KNUCKLES will spoil the beauty of an otherwise pretty hand, and when the swelling is not due to rheumatism or gout can be greatly reduced by painting each night with colourless iodine. The next morning the knuckles should be lightly massaged with a few drops of oil. When a slight stain on the hands does not matter for a day or two, tincture of iodine will be found more effective in reducing the swelling, but this leaves a brownish stain which lasts for a couple of days; it also makes the skin a little rough.

TOMATO JUICE will remove ink stains from the fingers and once in a while rub the cut half of a tomato over your sin. Let the juice dry on, then wash off with cold water. It bleaches the skin and is good for an acidity-blemished complexion.

YOUR NAILS

NAIL VARNISH, whether shell-pink, crimson, or natural expresses personality. And if you find that the little brushes supplied with the bottles don't "brush" so well, a good plan is to keep, in a bottle of nail polish remover, a very special one that's soft and puts on the varnish without a smear. Your brush will always be clean and ready for any colour. And, by the way, do remember that nothing clashes more than lipstick and nail polish of different reds. If you can't match them, see that your nails have a natural tint. You can't go wrong then!

NICOTINE STAINS on nails and fingers can be removed with eau-de-Cologne.

YOUR LEGS

TO REDUCE LEGS: If you are developing your calves to a disconcerting degree, get a pail of very hot water; into it put two handfuls of commercial salts and soak the legs in this for a quarter of an hour, topping up with more hot water, and more salts. You can treat arms the same way, and have a bath in it if you wish. It is definitely thinning.

TOO THICK ANKLES: Try this exercise. Rotate feet from ankle, curl toes tightly, unfurl and stretch, shaking the toes until they are relaxed.

SWOLLEN ANKLES: If the ankles swell and ache after a long walk, bandage them up with iodine ointment and rest them plenty.

KNEES: When you knees look and feel like a piece of sandpaper you should scrub them vigorously with a rubber brush and soapy lather until they feel softer. Cuticle remover is good for softening obstinate patches, too.

YOUR FEET

ZINC OINTMENT FOR THE FEET: Before a long tramp massage a little into the feet. This is soothing and healing, and good for any foot-ills, including soft corns.

SOLE: Give the soles a friction with Eau-de-Cologne, then plenty of talcum—it will make them feel like new feet.

BAREHEELS: Now that you are so often going stockingless, it matters so much that the backs of your heels should be smooth and pink and not have grey, hard lumps rubbed on them. Court shoes are the worst offenders, and if they don't grip, try the little heel-piece that can be inserted. Meanwhile get rid of the ugly lump itself by soaking your feet in warm water and rubbing at the lump gently with a well-soaped pumice from time to time—don't try to rub it away at once—and creaming it every night.

YOUR FIGURE

EXERCISING FOR BEAUTY: Even if you have to run about the house from morning till night and push the pram for miles daily, make certain of keeping your body young and supple and your system well aired by touching your toes twenty times a day and taking thirty deep breaths before an open window. The mid-morning break is a good time for this or when you get up after your afternoon nap, and I promise you the whole process won't take you more than ten minutes.

HOUSEWORK AND BEAUTY: The actual exercise involved in everyday housework is beneficial. The muscles are only healthily exercised in such domestic tasks as washing, bed-making and sweeping, but how to avoid the havoc wrought on hair and complexion by dust and dirt is always a problem for the busy housewife. The prudent one takes a few simple precautions. For instance:

Cover your hair with a neat cap or kerchief to keep it free from dust. To protect your complexion, smear a little cold cream over the face and neck ad wipe off with a cleansing tissue or soft handkerchief. Dust with oatmeal or good face powder. When housework is over, wash face in soft, warm water and the face will be beautifully soft and fresh.

WAIST (To keep slim): All body twisting movements are very good for keeping the waist slender. A roll of fat at and above the waistline in front can be reduced by repeating the two following exercises five times each way every day: (1) Stand erect, with feet together. Raise the arms above the head, finger tips touching. Bend down as far to the left as you can. Back to first position, then repeat to the right, keeping the abdomen, feet and the back well held in. (2) With the feet slightly apart and the hands above the head, the thumbs linked, move the body as far round as possible to the left, using the waist as pivot. Repeat swinging to the right. During the day always hold your ribs slightly above your waistline—this straightens your back and keeps the waist from thickening in front.

TUMMY EXERCISES: The best you can practice is lying on your back with the legs straight up, lowering each slowly in turn, also pedaling them in the air.

EXERCISE as often as you clean your teeth, if you want to keep your youthful figure. Stretching and bending, deep breathing, heels raising—you learned them all at school.

YOU'LL KEEP YOUR YOUTH—if you learn to relax. Nothing is more ageing than that look of strain which so often imprints your face when you're "chasing yourself" to get everything done at once. Five minutes quiet relaxation whenever you've the moment—sitting in the train, in the bus, on the way to work, waiting for a call on the telephone…will do wonders for you. Try not to think of anything for those brief moments; let your mind go limp if you're alone. Get to bed early o' nights.

PACKS (The method of self-treatment with face packs): (1) Tie a head-band round the hair to protect it, then proceed thoroughly to cleanse the face and throat with cream. (2) Remove the cream and apply more, then remove this completely. (3) Now apply the mask, smoothing it on in an upward direction, and lie down, with eyes closed for twenty minutes while it dries. (4)When the mask is hard and dry, remove it by holding a warm, damp towel over it and gently easing it off. (5) When the face is clear of pack, apply some almond emulsion or complexion milk all over the face and throat. (6) Wipe off with astringent lotion, and make up.

YEAST (For greasy skin): Milk is a good refiner of pores, and mixed with various ingredients, makes some lovely face masks which soothe—and nourish too. Here is one for the greasy skin. Mash some yeast to a creamy paste with a little milk and after cleansing the skin thoroughly apply the paste, avoiding the eyes, the brows and the hairline. Leave if for half an hour, then wash it off with warm water and splash on cold water as a finishing touch.

A PACK FOR A DRY, SALLOW SKIN: Most face packs can be used on a dry skin provided that (a) the skin is massaged with cream before and after the pack, and (b) the pack is let on the skin for five minutes less than the directions state, but here are two specially mild bleach packs for dry, sallow skin.

The first is made by mixing powdered magnesia to a thick, creamy paste with rose-water, and leaving it on the skin for fifteen minutes. Wash off with cold water.

The second is a bran and sour milk pack. Strain the liquid from the curd and add sufficient bran to make a thick paste. Smooth over the ace and wash off when dry.

EGG AND OIL MASH: Beat the yolks of two eggs till creamy, then add a few drops of olive oil, drop by drop, and an equal quantity of tincture of benzoin. Beat well again, then use.

OATMEAL PACK. This is used to soften and whiten the hands and should be applied about once a week to produce good results. Mix some fine oatmeal into a paste with strained lemon juice and peroxide of hydrogen in equal quantities. Spread the paste in equal quantities. Spread the paste evenly over the backs of the hands and leave it to dry.

SLEEP AND BEAUTY: Sufficient sleep is terribly important to beauty and a succession of bad nights spoils the looks more quickly than anything else I know. Aim at eight hours sleep each night, and if for any reason you have a broken night, organize your work so that you can make up the lost sleep during the day.

DIET FOR BEAUTY. The diet which makes for beauty is one which is low in starch—bread, sweets, pastry and rich in roughage such as skins of apples, pears and potatoes, cucumber and whole-wheat. Rich too in mineral salts and vitamins such as are found in fresh fruit, salads and vegetables, and in the case of calcium, so valuable for the teeth and nails, in milk, cheese and—dare I write it—orange juice. Take a large fresh salad every single day, a pint of vegetable stock, ½ pint of fresh milk, some cheese and the juice of an orange, when available. If, in addition to this, you eat wholemeal bread and shun strong tea and coffee, you can be sure that you are eating for beauty.

BEAUTY FOODS: "An apple a day keeps the doctor away," and if it does it also wards off blotches and all other forms of complexion blemishes. To obtain the best results, an apple should be taken fasting, before breakfast, and another just before going to bed.

"LETTUCE" BE BEAUTIFUL: Lettuce is a blood purifier and is excellent for those who suffer with spots and blotches. Do not add either vinegar or mayonnaise. A few drops of lemon juice added to olive oil is sufficient dressing.

TOMATOES: If the eyes appear dull and the whites are not as clear as you might wish, take a raw tomato with your breakfast. Do not add pepper or salt, for either of these reduces the beneficial effects of the tomato.

CARROTS: Those who are too pale and would like a

little natural colour in the cheeks should eat a few raw carrots every day. Choose young, soft carrots, scrape them and cut into very thin slices and eat as sandwiches between thin slices of brown bread and butter. A little cream cheese spread over the carrot will make the sandwich more tasty and cream cheese is also one of the greatest beauty foods.

RADISHES: The woman with a thin, fine skin which wrinkles early in life should try taking radishes for breakfast and tea. For the little fine lines around the eyes and mouth, these vegetables are excellent, and unless the wrinkles are very deep, five or six weeks will show a great improvement.

WATERCRESS is an easy way of taking iron and those who are in need of a tonic cannot do better than take a little watercress with one or two meals daily. It is also said that watercress is an antidote to the excessive use of tobacco.

BEAUTY BEVERAGES: Barley water: For a coarse, blotchy skin there is no better remedy than barley water taken regularly. At least a quart should be consumed every day and it is best to drink it half a pint at a time, between meals.

WATER—A BEAUTIFIER: Water is a tissue builder, and the woman who wishes to keep her skin firm and youthful should drink at least a quart of tap-water daily. The water should be taken, a half a pint at a time, between, not with, meals.

LEMONS FOR BEAUTY: Lemons are a great aid to beauty. The juice diluted with an equal quantity of rosewater, makes an excellent bleach for a discoloured neck; equal quantities of lemon juice, rosewater and glycerine whiten red, rough hands; the juice of a lemon added to the last rinsing water when shampooing the hair makes it bright and glossy and removes all traces of soap or shampoo powder, leaving it shining and smooth and very easy to wave.

The juice of a lemon in a glass of hot water taken first

thing in the morning, helps to reduce weight.

Used on the finger nails will remove stains, and applied to the cuticle in a glass of hot water first thing in the morning and last thing at night.

TO CLEAR A MUDDY COMPLEXION take a little lemon juice in a glass of hot water first thing in the morning and last thing at night.

MAKE-UP: The position of rouge on the cheeks must be decided by the bony structure of the face. A long face needs rouge shaded away from the nose and deeper towards the cheek bones, rather high up. A wide face needs the opposite treatment—the rouge deeper towards the nose, and not so high up. (2) Powder downwards to disguise hair and down. (3) Give eyebrow-pencilling a slight upward tilt at the outer corners for youth. (4) Keep make-up both natural and up-to-date.

THIS IS CHARM: Charm, that elusive quality which we women all long to possess, bulks most of us when we try to explain it, but recently I read a splendid definition: *Charm is nothing but vitality and the quality of not thinking eternally about oneself.*

Health

The Chief Essentials of Healthy Living can be Summarised as follows:—
1. A balanced diet.
2. Plenty of exercise and fresh air.
3. Adequate rest and sleep.
4. Personal Hygiene.
5. Avoidance of any focus of infection such as bad teeth, tonsils or sluggish digestive tract.

A BALANCED DIET: The relative daily quantities of the four main classes of foods, here outlined, are for a normal adult undergoing an average amount of physical exertion.

MEAT CLASS: 8 oz. meat foods, including butter, milk, cheese, eggs and fish.

BUTTER CLASS: From three and a half ozs. Butter and other fats.

BREAD CLASS: About 2 lbs. of bread or other foods made with flour and sugar, including some wholemeal.

FRUIT CLASS: Fresh fruit and canned or stewed fruit once a day.

VEGETABLE CLASS: From half to one pound of potatoes and other vegetables in addition, including some raw ones.

The different vitamins will "take care of themselves" in these classes, if fresh, natural foods are given precedence whenever possible.

Children need proportionately a larger quantity of the meat class than adults and not a great preponderance of the bread class.

THE MILKY WAY: Milk is such a hard and unobtrusive worker in the cause of health and beauty that sometimes it is over-looked. If you are too thin, drink a pint of creamy milk every day, and that look of not having enough flesh to cover your bones decently will soon disappear; what is more, the ragged nerves and exhaustion that usually accompanies underweight will also vanish. If you want to drink it, but fear for your figure, mix a glass of buttermilk with a glass of milk to lessen the proportion of fat. Buttermilk won't add an ounce of weight—milk helps to preserve your teeth, wards off chilblains and gives your body a large dose of health. Milk is an excellent internal "treatment." It happens to combine all the elements of a perfect food and yet doesn't overload the stomach. Green salad, brown bread and fruit, followed by a glass of milk is a perfect lunch. If you have milk for you "elevenses," take a biscuit with it. This tends to separate the particles in the milk and makes it more digestible.

KEEPING WELL IN WINTER-TIME: During foggy weather there always seems to be more illness than at any other time. It is a good plan to wear a thick, wide woollen scarf round the neck during this kind of weather, pulling it up over the mouth whenever possible. This will at least prevent you from breathing in the germ-laden air through your mouth. You should also carry a small box of throat pastilles in your bag. By sucking one of these occasionally—particularly in a crowded bus or train—you will be guarding yourself against infection. As soon as you return home you should gargle thoroughly to remove the last traces of fog from your throat. Cold, biting winds often produce headaches and neuralgia, and it is far better on such a day to wear a felt hat than a knitted cap or turban which provides little protection for the head.

Finally, if you want to keep fit in all weathers, never forget the value of all "heating" foods such as potatoes, sugar, honey, porridge, cream, butter, spaghetti, rice all dishes made with flour, also chocolate. These will help you to store up sufficient heat and energy to withstand the weather. When you are feeling cold and tired have a hot drink, such as coffee, meat extract in hot water, a hot fruit drink or hot milk.

YOUR DIET IN SPRING TIME: Start not to change your diet gradually; winter menus are too heavy for late spring and summer. Eat more salads, vegetables, egg and cheese dishes and less heating, starchy food.

KEEPING FIT FOR SUMMER TIME: Housework in really hot weather can be very exhausting unless we take steps to keep cool, both inside and out.

Diet is very important, very little meat should be eaten; cheese, eggs and fish can take its place. Plain water and fruit drinks should replace tea and coffee as often as possible. Avoid pork and bacon, all fats and too much bread and potatoes. Eat instead plenty of salads, fruit and vegetables. With regard to clothing: Light-coloured linens and cottons make the coolest garments.

Do not take cold baths, these will cool you for a short time, but later on you will feel warmer than ever. A tepid bath, on the other hand, will make you feel fresh and keep you cool.

WATER DRINKS: During hot weather, the body loses liquid quickly through perspiration. To help make up this loss, drink at least two full tumblers of water in addition to tea, coffee and other drinks during the day. Drink between meals.

REST AND QUIET, of which women require far more than they usually take. Periods of rest and quiet as well as 8 hours sound sleep at night are essential. If you are tired or suffering from lack of sleep, it is impossible for you to look your best. Try to close your eyes and relax completely on a comfortable couch even for ten minutes during the day.

TO KEEP A MEDICINE CHEST: (1) Bandages, in case of cuts and sprains; (2) Boracic Lint—for compresses; (3) Iodine, for immediate use in injuries; (4) Carron Oil—for burns; (5) Castor Oil—a strong aperient; (6) Boracic lotion—an antiseptic; (7) Sal Volatile—a stimulant, and useful for outward application in case of wasp stings, etc.; (8) Camphorated Oil; (9) Cascara Sagrada—a mild aperient; (10) A roll of adhesive, antiseptic plaster, in case of cuts, etc.; (11) Impecacuanha—an emetic; (12) Permanganate of Potash, in grains—for disinfecting purposes.

SUN AND YOUNG CHILDREN: Small children running about in the sun, should have a short coat to their sun-suit to give protection to back and shoulders. When the sun is high, make sure they wear a shady sun-hat or bonnet to protect the nape of the neck. Don't have a baby in a pram unprotected from glare. Keep his head well shaded and never let him lie with the sun in his eyes.

CURES

INDIGESTION: This often causes a sallow skin and spots. Greasy food as well as spicy ones should be avoided. A simple wholesome diet should be adopted with meat once a day at the most, and plenty of spring salads, fresh fruit and tomato juice. A glass of hot water first thing in the morning and last thing at night and between meals will be beneficial. If potatoes are eaten they should be baked in their jackets. Avoid strong tea, fresh bread, cakes and heavy puddings and some root vegetables (e.g., turnips) also twice-cooked meats. Take a course of magnesia tablets after meals.

CURES FOR CHILBLAINS: (1) Dissolve a little washing soda in a spoon over the fire or gas and during irritation state ply the liquid while hot and let it dry in; (2) Fill one bowl with cold water, another with nearly boiling water; plunge affected part in cold water and keep it there as long as can be borne, then into the hot water and so on alternatively till both waters are the same temperature; (3) In a small saucepan, bring to the boil 1 tablespoonful of new milk and 1 teaspoonful of powdered alum. When cold, rub well into chilblains, three times a day—Make fresh each day. This cure is only suitable for unbroken chilblains.

SPLINTER (To remove): The worst of getting a splinter into your flesh is that often the more you try to get it out the further you drive it in. Here is a way to bring it up to the surface painlessly: Put a little carbolic soap on some lint, lay it gently on the place and leave on for two hours; when you take it off you will find that the splinter has been drawn sufficiently from the flesh to be easily removed.

CHOKING REMEDY: If the patient is a child, turn him upside-down and slap smartly, but not too heavily on the back. In older people slap the back, or attempt to remove the obstruction from the back of the throat by inserting a finger. Take care not to bruise the throat passage.

WARTS: Wash and scrape a good-sized carrot, cut a slice off long ways and scoop out the inside, fill the cavity with ordinary salt and place the carrot in a saucer. In a short time juice will appear in the saucer, dap the warts with this regularly. It will not harm the skin.

CORN CURE: Here is a country cure for corns: Add a small quantity of potash to one eggcupful of sour milk, mix well, leave for five days. Then apply it to the corns.

FOR NEURALGIA: Put half a teaspoonful of neat brandy in the palm of the hand and draw it up the nose.

ONION POULTICE: An onion poultice beats all others for easing neuralgia or rheumatic pain; also sore throats.

TO RELIEVE SORE THROAT: (1) Gargle with

Epsom salts of the same strength as used for an aperients dose, to half a tumbler of hot water. This is comforting and cleansing; (2) Dip the second finger of right hand in dry bi-carbonate of soda and rub round your throat. This is said to prevent quinsy.

FOR STINGS IN MOUTH OR THROAT: Chew raw onion until doctor arrives. It is not necessary to swallow onion, but take a fresh slice from time to time and it will give great relief.

FOR ASTHMATIC SUFFERERS: Take a cup of boiling milk, into which stir a teaspoonful of pure glycerine. Drink when going to bed.

BALD PLACES ON HEAD: Remove the marrow from a bone, mix with a little Vaseline and apply nightly to bald parts.

HICCOUGH CURE: A tablespoonful of peppermint water is a simple and quick method of stopping hiccough.

CARE OF TEETH: Don't eat anything after you've cleaned your teeth at night. If you do, little bits of food will stick between your teeth and have the whole night undisturbed in which to start a rot. Do remember your gums. If they are pink and firm they are probably all right. If they are white and spongy, massage them with the tip of your finger or your toothbrush dipped in common salt. Keep your gums healthy by rubbing them with a toothbrush dipped in a little salt and water every day. This friction will stimulate the circulation of the blood.

TO CLEAN ARTIFICIAL TEETH: Dissolve a dessertspoonful of Epsom salts in a tumbler of warm water and scrub the dental plate in it.

FOOT CARE

FRESH FEET: To keep the feet healthy, happy and fresh-smelling, they must be washed and carefully dried every 24 hours, and if possible, dusted with talc. Clean stockings every day, and two pairs of shoes, worn alternatively and aired in between are other "musts." If the feet perspire easily, try bathing them with a weak solution of permanganate of potash.

TO PREVENT BLISTER on the heels, rub soap on.

PREPARE YOUR FEET FOR A LONG WALK by rubbing in Eau-de-Cologne or methylated spirits, rub damp soap over the backs of the heels, and dust quickly with talc.

CURE FOR CORNS, HARD SKIN, ETC.: Equal parts of glycerine and methylated spirits mixed together and rubbed well into the feet night and morning will banish corns, hard skin and even bunions.

Dress

Dress sense matters more than ever; because if blessed with it you can look nicer and feel "good" from top to toe on the smallest outlay.

Under the present conditions none of us expect to be covered with fine feathers, but whilst endeavouring to economise we must try not to let our appearance reflect the times.

Here are some important points that will help the all-important matter of looking your best, and cost practically nothing.

Keep your hair, teeth and nails scrupulously clean. See that your hair parting, stocking seams and show heels are straight.

Use your clothes brush frequently; the nicest "rig" is spoilt by stray hairs lying around collar and shoulders.

Be equally careful of things that don't show as of the things that do show.

See that your shoes shine brilliantly and your nose doesn't. Finally and most important of all: seen that the back of your neck hasn't unsightly, bearded effect. Points that sound trivial but are so important.

HOSE SENSE: Keep colours fresh with a few drops of vinegar in the rinsing water.

Rub a candle over the heels and toes to get stockings to give harder wear.

Another way of staving off holes in the toe is to change the stockings on to alternate feet each day. This ensures that the portion which has had the greatest strain one day is eased on the second. The simplest way to know one from the other is to arrange them at night over the back of a chair in the order you want to wear them next day.

RAINDROPS SPOTTING SILK STOCKINGS: Rainy weather plays havoc with silk stockings, but if three or four drops of methylated spirits are put in the last rinsing water, when washing, there will be no spotty marks caused by raindrops on the stockings.

CARE OF RAYON STOCKINGS: Rayon stockings need proper treatment in order to make sure they will give the longest possible wear. Always wash new rayon stockings before wearing them. Use lukewarm water and soap after washing. Dip the stockings in lukewarm water again after wearing them—every time. And don't forget that rayon fabric temporarily loses strength while it is wet, so handle wet stockings carefully and don't put them on again for 24 hours at least. They should be dried slowly away from direct exposure to the heat of a fire.

BEST METHOD OF STORING SILK STOCKINGS: Steep in cold water, then rinse in tepid water. Dry in open air. Do not dry at fire. When thoroughly aired put into air-tight jars.

SHOES AND BOOTS

WHEN BUYING NEW SHOES, don't forget that light-coloured shoes make large feet look larger, whilst dark shoes make them look small and trim. Shining surfaces *such as patent leather and satin* are also unsuitable in bigger sizes, as are laced-up shoes, brogues with tongues, and open-work sandals.

Suede, dull kid, or calf shoes will also help to make large feet look neater and smaller. If you wear court shoes, remember that the shorter the front of the shoe the shorter your feet will look.

TO CLEAN SUEDE SHOES: First of all, stuff the shoes full of soft paper, then have ready a saucer filled with spirits of turpentine and apply a little of this to the shoes with a clean rag. Keep rubbing them and turning the rag till the shoes look clean. Then hang them up to dry where there is a current of air till the smell of turpentine has vanished. This will make the shoes look quite new again.

TO STORE: Shoes that are not in use should be cleaned at least once a fortnight, if nit they will wear out almost as much as if worn every day. Thick winter boots should have a little castor oil or other grease rubbed in occasionally when not in use.

New boots and shoes improve by being kept a short time before they are worn. Don't be too liberal with polish when cleaning them as it's apt to dry on and cake, preparing the way for cracks.

NEW BOOTS AND SHOES will last much longer if they are given a coat of copal varnish on the soles, then left to dry thoroughly before wearing.

TO BLACKEN BROWN SHOES: To make shabby brown shoes look like good black ones, first rub with the cut side of a raw potato and then polish with a mixture of equal quantities of blue-black ink and ordinary blacking.

OLD BROWN SHOES: To clean and freshen up old worn, faded, brown leather shoes: Clean and brush well, then rub in a little red ink, let dry and polish with the ordinary polish and you have them as good as new.

SHABBY TOECAPS: The toecaps of shoes which have become worn and shabby, will look like new and take a very good polish if brushed over with gum and allowed to dry before polishing.

DAMPSHOES: Damp shoes will polish well if a little paraffin is added to the cleaning paste.

TO MAKE BOOTS AND SHOES RESIST WET and

snow: two parts beeswax to one of mutton fat, mix well and apply to the boots at night.

DRY POLISH (To soften): When a tin of shoe polish gets hopelessly dry, add a little vinegar to it and you will be able to put the polish on your shoes quite easily.

TO CLEAN TENNIS SHOES: Tennis shoes can be cleaned quickly if wanted in a hurry by mixing the cleaner with methylated spirit instead of water.

TO REPAIR TENNIS SHOES: Wide adhesive tape will often prevent the soles and uppers of plimsoles and tennis shoes from parting company.

IF THE TIPS OF YOUR SHOE LACES COME OFF dip the ends in melted sealing wax. Shape to a point with the fingers while the wax is still warm.

WELLINGTONS: When children wear wellington boots in wet weather sprinkle a small quantity of talcum powder inside. This prevents the rubber from "drawing" the feet and doesn't harm the hosiery.

SHINE ON CLOTH: Cloth that has become shiny in places can be renovated by brushing lightly with a clothes brush dipped in a mixture of equal parts of methylated spirit and water to which a tablespoonful of ammonia has been added. Then iron lightly under damp muslin.

MAN'S HAT (To prevent grease mars): If a strip of thin blotting paper is placed inside the lining-band of a man's light-coloured hat, and renewed when necessary, the hat will never show grease marks on the outside caused by brilliantine, etc. on the hair.

INVERTED PLEATS: To keep inverted pleats in place fix hair grips round the hem of a skirt after hanging it up.

A DRESS-HANGER HINT: When you hang a sleeveless dress on a hanger, nearly always one shoulder at once slips off, and the dress falls in a heap on the floor, which is most irritating. To prevent this, take two fairly large corks and nail one each end of the hanger; bind round with ribbon or silk to match the covering of the hanger and you won't have any more trouble.

SHINE ON ROUGH OR FLUFFY MATERIAL such as skirts and coats which have become shiny through wear can have the shine taken off by light rubbing with an old piece of emery paper.

DUSTPROOF COVER: A dust-proof cover for your little girl's best frock is easily made from a pillow case. Cut a hole in the centre of the closed end, just big enough to allow the hook of the hanger go through. Slip the dress on the hanger; button up the ends of the case—and there you are.

PRESERVE OVER-SHOES AND GOLOSHES through the summer by giving them an occasional rub over with a little oil. Stuff them with discarded socks or screws of paper to prevent cracks and store them in a good dry place.

PERFUME: What perfume shall be used must be left to individual choice. Some prefer a heavy Oriental scent, others the delicate fragrance of fresh flowers. In this matter it is best to study one's personality. The exotic-looking women will be wise to choose some scent that will accord with her type, and the young girls should decide on a flower scent which will suit their fresh youthfulness.

SACHETS—ECONOMICAL: You can save money on your favourite scent sachets if you make a note of this idea. Cut up some squares of blotting paper and sprinkle some of your favourite perfume on these. They will last fresh for some time and, of course, they can be renewed at no expense.

TO DECANT: You may not have a suitable funnel to decant scent into a spray. Take a clean, empty egg shell, make a little hole in it with a thick needle and the scent will filter through without any waste.

TO PERFUME HANDKERCHEIFS: If you like a faint perfume from your handkerchiefs, dissolve a few bath crystals in the final rinsing water when you wash them.

TO REVIVE AN OLD FELT HAT: Place the hat over the spout of a kettle half full of boiling water so that the steam is forced through the felt, place over a basin or hat mould to dry, then brush briskly with a stiff brush. Replace on trimming and renew the head lining.

FOR ANKLE SOCKS: Garters worn under the turnovers of ankle socks will prevent them from slipping under the heel and keep them tidy.

GLOVES (To dye): You can dye your gloves quite easily with a good suede dye. Give the gloves one coat and allow it at least twenty-four hours in which to dry thoroughly, then give a second coat. Brush the gloves thoroughly after this coat is dry and the gloves will look perfect.

FURS: Remember, before wearing a fur at any time, always to give it a gentle shaking. This will make it wear and look much better.

Recipes

TEA-CAKES: Take 1 lb. of flour, 2 ozs. Sultanas, 1 oz mixed peel, 1 level teaspoonful of mixed spice, 1½ teaspoonfuls of bread soda, 2 large tablespoonfuls of castor sugar, 2 ozs. butter, 1 egg, ½ pint buttermilk or sour milk. Method: Rub butter into flour, mix in all dry ingredients. Add buttermilk to the well-beaten egg, make a well in centre of mixture, pour in egg and milk; mix to a firm dough; cut into round cakes about an inch deep and bake on a floured tin in a hot over for 15 minutes.

WHEN EGGS ARE SCARCE the following eggless recipes should prove helpful:

LUNCH CAKE: Three ozs. of butter, three ozs. sugar, one tablespoonful marmalade, half pound flour, quarter pound raisins (if procurable), quarter pint of milk and one and a half teaspoons soda.

Cream the butter and sugar, add the marmalade and beat up well. Add the flour and the raisins alternately with the soda dissolved in the milk. Bake in a shallow tin for three-quarters of an hour in a moderate oven.

CHEESE SAUCE: Make a white sauce in the usual manner and when cooked, add to it two or three tablespoons of grated cheese; use for coating cauliflowers or other vegetables. If convenient, sprinkle a little cheese on top and brown lightly in the oven.

CHEESE DREAMS: Cut two slices of bread, not too thick, spread thinly with butter. Grate some cheese on bread and if you happen to have a little made mustard spread on the other side, but it can be done without. Sandwich together; press firmly; cut into four; fry in hot fat till golden brown both sides. Serve at once.

CHEESE DISH: *Ingredients*: 2 tomatoes; 2 eggs; 2 ozs. butter. *Method*: Melt butter in frying pan. Add tomatoes, cut in small pieces and fry for three or four minutes. Beat eggs with milk and pour into frying pan among tomatoes. Keep moving with large spoon till egg is no longer in liquid form. Add grated cheese. Fry for two minutes ore. Serve on hot-buttered toast.

POTATO AND CHEESE CROQUETTES: Left-over mashed potato can be made into a tasty dish in this way for lunch or supper or meatless days. Mashed potatoes can be mixed with half the quantity of grated cheese and seasoned with salt and pepper. An egg can also be added if desired. Make into little rolls, turn in bread crumbs and fry until crisp and brown.

COFFEE BUNS: Mix 4 ozs. self-raising flour with 1 oz. sugar, rub in 1 oz. butter and pour on this 1 egg with ½ teaspoon coffee essence. Add a little milk for mixing, then bake in containers or in a flat tin in a quick oven.

FLAVOURED BREAD: When baking bread, make a special small loaf. When kneading it place a piece of cheese in the middle. Then pop it in the oven and bake in the usual way. The hot oven melts the cheese and it is quite a novelty cut into slices and spread with butter.

BISCUITS

KRACK-A-JACK: One teaspoonful ratafia essence, 8 ozs. Quaker oats or flake meal, 4 ozs. butter, 4 ozs. sugar (brown, if you can get it), ¼ teaspoonful of bicarbonate of soda dissolved in a dessertspoonful of hot water. *Method*: Melt the butter and sugar in a pan, add oats, soda and ratafia. Bake in a greased, deep tin in a moderate oven for

1 hour. Cut into squares and dust with sugar.

OATMEAL BISCUITS: Mix together four ozs. of flour and three of oatmeal with half a teaspoonful of baking powder, a pinch of salt and two ozs. of sugar. Melt three ozs. of butter and mix it with the other ingredients, adding sufficient warm milk and water to make a workable dough. Roll out and bake in a moderate oven for ten minutes. (By omitting the sugar and using less butter in this recipe you have the perfect biscuit for savoury spreads or cheese). Or if you want something really delicious for tea spread each biscuit with jam and finish off with a layer of stiffly-whipped cream.

PASTRY

POTATO PASTRY: 4 ozs. mashed potatoes, 4 ozs. flour, 3 ozs. butter, 1 teaspoonful of baking powder. Rub the butter into flour until finely crumbled. Add baking powder, then mix in potatoes. Add sufficient water to make a stiff dough. Roll out thinly. This pastry is suitable for savoury or sweet dishes.

PASTRY WITHOUT FAT: Mix together 8 ozs. of wheatmeal flour, level teaspoonful of baking powder, a pinch of salt. Stir in nearly ¼ pint of cold milk or milk and water. Roll out and use. This pastry must be eaten hot.

SPICED APPLE PASTRY: Roll out thinly some pastry; spread half of it with grated apple, a few chopped raisins and one teaspoonful of spice. Fold over other half of pastry, press lightly with rolling pin. Wipe over with warm water and lightly sprinkle with sugar. Place in flat bang tin, mark into squares. Equally good hot or cold.

EGG PATTIES: 6 eggs, 1 oz. chopped ham, 3 or 4 chopped mushrooms (can be omitted), pepper and salt, short pastry. *Method*: Line some deep patty tins with pastry. Drop an egg gently into each. Put a little ham and mushroom on each and cover with a round of pastry. Season. Bake at a temperature of 450 deg. for 15 minutes.

LUNCH OR SUPPER DISHES

HAM BALLS: Ingredients: ½ lb. cold potatoes, 2 ozs minced ham or bacon, 1 oz. butter, 1 egg, seasoning, a little milk or cream, egg, bread crumbs. *Method*: Sieve the potatoes and add the meat, butter, one well-beaten egg and seasoning. Add sufficient milk or cream to enable you to form into small balls; egg and bread crumb them, and fry in boiling fat to a golden brown.

CORNED BEEF OR HAM SCRAMBLE: 6 ozs. of corned beef or ham, 1 tablespoonful of bacon fat or butter, 3 eggs, pepper to taste, rounds or squares of buttered toast, 1 teaspoon each of minced chives and parsley. Beat eggs slightly in a basin. Melt fat in a saucepan. Add chopped corned beef or ham. Cook for 2 or 3 minutes, stirring frequently. Stir in eggs. Season to taste with pepper. Serve on buttered toast, or, if preferred, in a ring of fried sliced apples or potatoes enough for six persons. To vary this recipe serve each portion garnished with peeled, sliced, fried mushrooms or tomatoes.

COTTAGE PIE: Cottage pie made with a "Roof" of potatoes and turnips cooked together, then mashed, is a welcome change.

TRY THIS EASY RECIPE: Combine ¾ lb. minced beef, ¼ lb. minced ham and a ½ cup of soft bread crumbs. Mix together 1 slightly-beaten egg, 1 teaspoon salt and 1 teaspoon pepper. Blend egg and meat mixtures and form into medium-sized meat balls. Brown in a hot greased frying pan. Open a tin of beans and turn into a casserole. Add ½ cup of ketchup and one teaspoon meat sauce and combine lightly. Top with browned meat balls, and heat in a hot oven 100 deg. Far., 20 minutes or until piping hot.

LEFT-OVER SCRAPS OF MEAT: Chop or mince the meat left on the bones, put it in a pan with two eggs, add a knob of butter and seasoning and stir until the mixture thickens; or pot by putting scraps through a mincer; season and mix to a paste with butter.

CHEESE

CHEESE IT: Dieticians tell us the importance of eating cheese for its value as a protective food. So let's all put cheese on our daily menu and to help you to do so here are some recipes for lunch or supper dishes: *Ingredients*: 1 teacupful of grated cheese, 1 tablespoonful of butter, 1 cup milk, 2 eggs, toast. *Method*: Add cheese to the milk and cook until it becomes a cream; add eggs when well beaten; also butter, salt and pepper. Stir for a few minutes on fire. Serve on hot toast.

EGGS

TOMATO FRITTERS: Here is a recipe that will help you to economise with eggs and yet give your family some of their essential vitamins. Make a thick pancake batter, using one egg to ¼ lb. flour, pinch of salt, large teacupful of milk. Beat well and leave for at least an hour. It can be made the night before, if convenient. Slice some tomatoes, dip in batter, coat well. Fry in hot bacon fat and serve with a little grilled or fried bacon.

SCRAMBLED EGGS are a tasty dish, but eggs are expensive. Get over the difficulty by making one egg do the duty of two. The following recipe will be found very satisfactory: 1 egg, ½ oz. of cornflour, ½ oz. butter (or margarine in normal times). Mix the cornflour with milk, add the beaten egg and season; add parsley. Melt butter and add the blended cornflour and egg to it. Heat and serve on buttered toast at once or on mashed potato.

ONE EGG WILL GO AS FAR AS TWO at breakfast time if you beat it, then stir it into a smoothly-mashed, cold boiled potato. Beat well together, then fry with the breakfast bacon, or by itself, in hot fat, dropping it into the pan in tablespoonfuls.

SAUSAGES.

SAUSAGE MEAT: If pastry is hard to come by and you want sausage rolls, you can wrap uncooked sausage meat in mashed potato and bake this in the oven to make a sort of imitation sausage roll. Sausage meat can also be mixed with mashed potato in whatever proportion you like and fried in little cakes, this will make it go further.

BOILED SAUSAGES: If you find fried or grilled sausages at all indigestible, try boiling them in a pan of hot water, using just enough to cover them. Bring this water slowly to the boil. Then simmer them very gently for 40 minutes. The secret of success here lies in the very slow cooking.

A GOOD FILLING FOR SAVOURY PUDDINGS can be made from forcemeat balls, sausage meat shaped into walnuts, and some sliced, mixed vegetables all moistened with a thick brown gravy.

POTATOES

POTATO SCONES: 6 or 8 potatoes freshly boiled in salted water then passed through a potato masher. Beat in ½ oz. butter, turn out on a floured board and work in as much flour as the potatoes will take—the dough should be very light and springy. Roll out thinly, shape into larger rounds, cut these into four, prick, place on hot griddle. Cook 3 minutes on each side and serve with hot butter—these are really good.

BAKED POTATO CHIPS: The shortage of fat for deep frying has deprived many of us of our chip potatoes. Here is a simple substitute. Peel the potatoes and cut them lengthways into eight or so "quarters." Let these lie for an hour in cold water, then dry them well in a cloth, and brush each over with melted dripping. Then put them into a greased baking tin or dish, and bake them in a hot oven, turning them over and over.

POTATO BUTTER: Mix equal quantities of dripping and cold, mashed potatoes, add a pinch of salt.

POTATO PANCAKES: You'll like potato pancakes! Mash five or six potatoes, add two tablespoons flour and seasoning and mix with an egg and a little milk. Roll out to about ¼ inch thick, fry both sides in dripping and serve rolled up.

SOUP

THE STOCK POT: For three parts of the year at any rate, every good housewife should keep a stock pot going. Into it must go every scrap of meat and bone that might otherwise be thrown away, and with it good nourishing soup can be provided at any time, at the most trifling cost. Every evening the contents of the stock pot should be turned into an earthenware crock; and once in twenty-four hours the stock pot must be brought to the boil. With these precautions a stock pot will go indefinitely, bones being strained from it when all the goodness has been extracted from them.

CELERY SOUP: 1 head of celery, 1 quart stock, 1 onion, 1 tablespoonful cornflour, half pint milk, pepper and salt. Thoroughly wash and clean the celery and cut into pieces. Peel and slice the onion and out into the saucepan with the stock and celery. Season with salt and pepper and bring to the boil, then simmer slowly for two hours. Run through a sieve. Mix the cornflour with the milk to a smooth paste and add to the soup. Boil again for five minutes.

FIVE-MINUTE SOUP: *Ingredients*: ½ pint of milk and water, cupful mashed potatoes, one tablespoon of tomato sauce or 1 small onion, grated, lump of butter or fat size of walnut, pepper and salt to taste. Boil milk and potatoes for five minutes; add tomato sauce, seasoning and the butter to serve.

SOUP THAT IS TOO SALTY: Soups in which bacon or ham bones are boiled are likely to be too salty. This may be considerably overcome if a whole potato is put in with the bones. Do not eat the potato.

VEGETABLES
HERE IS A PRACTICAL ECONOMICAL DISH,

making a tasty and nourishing dinner, suited to simple resources:

Fill a pie dish with uncooked, sliced potatoes and finely-sliced onions in layers, sprinkling each layer with a little chopped parsley and adding a rasher or two of streaky bacon cut in strips. Fill the pie dish three-quarters full of milk and put some bits of butter on top. Bake for fully an hour in a moderate oven and allow to brown thoroughly before serving.

JAKEEN'S PIE: Put part of a tin of beans in a pie dish, add a layer of crumbs, pepper, salt and a little mustard. Cover with grated cheese, then with thick layer of mashed potatoes. Bake three-quarters of an hour in a moderate oven until nicely brown. Serve piping hot. If a larger pie is required the whole tin of beans must be used.

GREEN PEAS FRITTERS: One medium tin of Batchelor peas or equivalent of cooked, dried peas, one teaspoonful dried mint, one cupful bread crumbs, one medium onion, pinch of sage and salt. Chop and fry onion, mash peas. Add all other ingredients and form into rissoles. Roll in flour and fry until crisp and brown.

FISH

FISH CAKES: ½ lb. cold fish finely chopped. ½ lb. mashed potatoes, 1 teaspoonful of finely-chopped parsley, pepper, salt, 1 egg. Mix all these ingredients together, flour the hands and form into round cakes ½ an inch deep. Fry in hot fat; drain and serve on a dish garnished with parsley.

FISH ON TOAST: *Ingredients*: ½ lb. smoked fillet, 1 egg, 1 oz. butter, 1 small cup of milk, seasoning. Cook fish in milk and water for five minutes. Flake fish, add beaten egg, butter, milk and seasoning. Put all into saucepan, stir mixture until it thickens and serve spread on hot buttered toast.

HERRING PASTIES: This is rather an uncommon dish. Clean the fresh herrings, take out their back bones and stuff with sausage meat. Put each one into a pastry pasty, with the heads ad tail sticking out at each end. Half an hour each will see them done.

PUDDINGS AND SWEETS

FRUIT WHIPS: 3 tablespoonfuls fruit puree (passed through a sieve), 1 egg white, large, or two small, sugar to taste. *Method*: Whip white of egg till stiff. Add gradually to the cold, sweetened pulp, beating all the time until very stiff. Use fairly thick puree, drain off unnecessary juice. Serve cold with sponge cake or plain sweet biscuits.

MELLOW APPLE CREAM: Peel, core and grate eating apples according to quantity required. Mix quickly with sweetened condensed milk. Heaped into a dish this makes a delicious sweet which children especially love.

A QUICKLY-MADE PUDDING: This makes a good, substantial pudding which can cook while eating the first course; apples, rhubarb, or any quick-cooking fruit can be used. Put fruit in saucepan, cover with water, sweeten and flavour to taste and bring to boil. Add small suet dumplings—approximately two tablespoonfuls of flour and one teaspoonful of suet is enough for each person.

GOOSEBERRY CHARLOTTE: 2 lb. gooseberries; ½ lb. sugar; ½ oz. gelatine; 1 teacup hot water; small sponge cakes; whipped cream. Cook the fruit and sugar to a pulp, pass through a sieve and add the gelatine dissolved in hot water. Line a mould with slices of the sponge cake and pour the puree in the centre. Cool, turn on to a glass dish and serve with whipped cream.

ORANGE CUSTARD: Peel some oranges, discarding pips and pith. Cut into slices and sweeten to taste, place in a dish, pour over thick, boiled custard. Serve cold.

GOOSEBERRY TRIFLE PLATTER: Odd slices of bread, if not used up for toast, etc., can be made into this sweet:

Cut bread into fingers, after removing crusts. Piece together into a round, covering the centre of a dinner plate. Sprinkle with juice from stewed gooseberries.

Completely cover with thick custard; top this all over with a single layer of stewed gooseberries which have been cooked slowly to keep them whole, left till cold, drained.

SANDWICHES

SANDWICH PASTE: Grate up your dry ends of cheese to make a grand savoury sandwich filling. To every 2 ozs. cheese add a pinch of grated nutmeg and a few drops of Worcester or any meat sauce and work into it nearly 1 oz. butter, press into a jar, cover with melted fat and tie down.

SANDWICHES: Neat oblong slices of bread, with crusts removed and quickly fried a light golden brown are good, spread with 2 or 3 spoonfuls of hot mince; clap on the covering toast and serve quickly.

SWEET SANDWICHES: The ideal sweet sandwich is formed of a tiny scone, split and spread with a little preserve, which is then covered with a teaspoonful of whipped cream. Put on the top and it is ready. There must be put together just before tea-time.

SOMETHING SAVOURY FOR TEA: Open a jar of fish or meat paste, spread it on fingers of fried bread after cooling it and give it a thin cap of chopped olive or parsley.

MARMALADES AND JAMS

"WAR-MALADE"—Double marmalade: Stew 2 lbs. apples with sufficient water to prevent burning, very little sugar, add 2 lbs. marmalade. Boil few minutes, stirring all the time. Turn into warm jars.

MARMALDE THAT CAN BE MADE FROM ONLY THE PEELS OF ORANGES AND LEMONS: the pulp itself is not required. *Method*: two-thirds fill a 4 lb. jam jar with water. Add the shredded rinds of 6 oranges and one lemon, then fill the jar to full capacity with water. Leave standing three to six days, then turn into saucepan and boil for one hour with lid on (this is very important).

Remove from heat. Add three pounds of sugar, stir until dissolved. Return from heat. Add three pounds of sugar, stir until dissolved. Return to heat and boil for about 1½ to 1¾ hours. Test on plate. *Note*: the orange rinds may be added to jar day by day as they become available. It is not necessary to use the six oranges at once.

IF YOUR MARMALADE OR JAM HAS NOT THICKENED SUFFICIENTLY GET A SQUARE OF JELLY (lemon or orange flavour for marmalade, any flavour you like for the jam) and put the whole square into preserving pan with your preserves. Bring to the boil and stir until the jelly is dissolved. You will be delighted with the result. It will set just as it should be and the flavour of your preserves will be greatly improved.

APPLES: Don't throw away apple-peelings; boil them down and to every pint of liquid allow 1 lb. sugar. Boil till it sets. Try it on a saucer before potting.

THIS AND THAT

SPECIAL RECIPE FOR GOOD COFFEE: Into a previously-warmed earthenware jug place three heaped dessertspoons of fresh coffee to each pint; pour boiling water, stir well, and leave to stand for five minutes.

BROWNING FOR COLOURING GRAVIES, STEWS, ETC.: Put two or three ozs. sugar and two tablespoons of water into an iron frying pan, let it melt and when it becomes a nice brown colour, add ½ pint of boiling water, boil up and stir. Let it stand at side of fire until sugar is melted; cool and keep in a well-corked bottle.

SUBSTITUTE FOR CREAM: ½ pint milk, 1 teaspoonful cornflour, 1 teaspoonful sugar, 1 oz. butter, Vanilla essence. Make cornflour into a smooth paste with a little of the milk. Bring remainder of milk to the boil, add butter, sugar and a few drops of vanilla essence, cook until thick (about 5 mins.) Beat with an egg whisk until cold. Result—splendid substitute for fresh cream.

MIXED CANDIED PEEL: Remove the peel from 4

or 5 oranges and lemons and soak it in salt water for about 4 days or longer, if convenient; then boil the peel in fresh water until soft. Add 2 lbs. of castor sugar to every pint of water in which the peel has been boiled, and boil again until the liquid becomes sugary. Remove and drain until the peel is quite cool.

GREEN TOMATO CHUTNEY: 2 lbs. green tomatoes, 2 medium-sized onions, thinly sliced, 1 large tablespoonful salt, 4 ozs. seedless raisins, cut small, 6 ozs. moist sugar, 1 teaspoonful dry mustard, 1 teaspoonful ground ginger, a pinch of cayenne pepper, ¾ pint vinegar. Wash and dry tomatoes and cut in thick slices; put them in layers in a bowl with sliced onions and salt between and leave 12 hours. Mix the mustard and ginger with a little of the tomato liquor and turn all into a stewpan with the rest of the ingredients. Stir well with a wooden spoon as the chutney heats, and simmer gently until it is soft and thick—about the consistency of hot apple jam. Let cool a little, then pour into wide-mouthed jars that have heated for a minute or two. When the chutney is cold, cover jar to make air-tight. If in doubt about covers, pour a little clarified mutton fat on top of chutney. If using screw-on tops with rubbers, cover jars with a greaseproof paper before screwing down lid. A further precaution is to seal joint between metal tops and glass with adhesive paper hand. If unable to obtain raisins, substitute just-ripe plums or apple—about six ounces. If no moist sugar, you may use the ordinary.

PICKLED BEETROOT: Small beetroots, boiled till tender, left to cool, then pared and sliced into a jar and covered with mild vinegar that has been boiled two or three minutes and left to become quite cold again, are very good. A little pepper and salt, and a slice or two of onion added to the vinegar improve the pickle. Tie down carefully to completely exclude air.

Cookery Hints

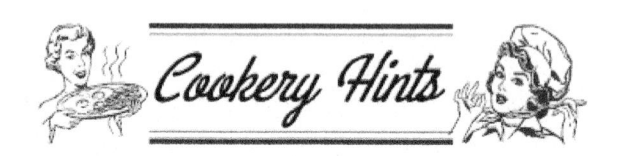

ABOUT VEGETABLES:

(1) They should be prepared and cooked the day they are wanted for the table—not before.

(2) To bring out the flavour, always add salt to the water in which they are cooked—about one teaspoonful to each quart of water.

(3) All green vegetables and most others should be plunged in fast-boiling water and cooked rather rapidly until done. New potatoes—boiling water. Old potatoes—cold water.

(4) To avoid the smell of boiling cabbage, cauliflowers, onions, etc., drop a piece of toasted bread or crust in with them.

(5) Once vegetables are cooked they should be served at once—they should on no account be allowed to stand, "keeping hot," for long.

(6) Long, slow cooking and especially keeping hot, destroys the vitamins in greens.

WHEN COOKING VEGETABLES: All vegetables grown above the ground should be boiled with the lid off the saucepan, while those grown under should have the lid kept on.

SPROUTS: A good and quick idea for shredding sprouts is

to shred them with a sharp knife, then steam them. They take only about ten to fifteen minutes to cook this way.

POTATOES

ROASTED POTATOES: You can't call yourself a cook until you've turned out roasted potatoes with a crisp, brown outer crust, and a soft, white inner core. The whole secret lies in drying them carefully after peeling and popping into a baking tin of boiling fat in the oven, ¼ hour before you put in the joint. It may sound simple enough to you, but it makes all the difference.

FAST POTATO SCRAPING: First soak a short time in cold water (while doing other jobs). Then always scrape from the stalk end of the potato. The skin and eyes will come off much more easily.

FRYING POTATOES: If you are frying potatoes, first cut them into fingers, then soak them in cold water for thirty minutes. Drain and dry in a clean cloth and then plunge them into boiling fat that is quite still.

BAKED POTATOES: Did you know that you could have baked potatoes without lighting the oven? Boil the potatoes in their jackets until they are cooked but not too soft, then drain off the water and bake them slowly under the grill, turning constantly.

WHEN BAKING POTATOES IN THEIR SKINS brush them over first with salad oil before placing them in the oven and they will be crisp and tender instead of leathery.

CHIPPED POTATOES: If you sprinkle a little baking powder in the boiling fat in which chipped potatoes are fried the chips will be beautifully crisp and brown.

TINY NEW POTATOES, so often thrown away, can be used (and the trouble of peeling them saved) in this way: Wash them well, dry them, and cook them just as they are in deep fat.

CARROTS

TO MAKE CARROT TEA: Take a few good carrots, size immaterial; grate them on a fine bread grater; place on a dry tin or frying pan and put it on top of a hot range. Keep the shredded material turned with a fork or spoon until all moisture has evaporated. If the result is not sufficiently dried out as to make it "tea" of a colour almost resembling the imported commodity, the tin may be placed in a hot oven until it has attained a crispness.

TO CLEAN YOUNG CARROTS rub them with a coarse, dry cloth, sprinkled with kitchen salt.

CARROTS CAN BE BAKED ROUND THE JOINT in the same way as potatoes, *artichokes* and *parsnips*.

DANDELIONS: Young dandelion leaves make an admirable salad and they can be cooked in the same way as spinach.

NETTLES (but they must be young), can be cooked in the same way.

PARSLEY: The flavour and juice of parsley will be preserved very much if washed in warm water instead of cold.

BEETROOT: Beetroot will keep fresh for quite a long time if a little mustard is mixed with vinegar poured over it.

TO PREVENT BEETROOT FROM "BLEEDING": Seal ends with red-hot poker before cooking in boiling water.

LETTUCE

THE OUTER LEAVES of lettuce have more vitamin value than the heart—so remove only the withered leaves. Try serving lettuce shredded and mixed with chives and dressing.

TO MAKE LETTUCE CRISP put a pinch of powdered borax into the water in which you wash it. Let it soak for half an hour in this, then shake it free from water; wipe each half separately, after well rinsing and you will be delightful with the crispness of the lettuce. Salted water softens lettuce, but borax both cleans and freshens it.

USE THE OUTSIDE LEAVES of lettuce in soup.

CELERY: If you wish to keep celery crisp for a few days after it has been cleaned ready for table, place a lump of sugar in the glass with it. Then, when you wish to serve it again, rinse well in clean, cold water.

TO TEST MUSHROOMS: To solve the difficult problem of whether your mushrooms are really mushrooms, stir them with a silver spoon while cooking them. If there are toadstools lurking among them, the silver will become discoloured.

MUSHROOMS WILL NOT SHRIVEL UP in cooking if first dipped in boiling water.

TOMATOES

GREEN TOMATOES: When the weather has become too cold for your outdoor tomatoes do not pick them; instead cut the whole plant close to the root and hang upside down in a dark cupboard with a paper underneath to catch any tomatoes that falloff. This ripens green tomatoes and keeps them fresh and you will be picking ripe ones up to Christmas.

TO RIPEN GREEN TOMATOES: Pack the tomatoes in bran, if procurable; alternatively, wrap in brown paper and leave in a warm place. Time varies considerably. Some will ripen in a week, others four or five weeks. Give them their own time.

IF TOMATOES ARE USED FOR SANDWICHES or salads, cut with a bread-saw instead of a knife. Slices can be cut very thinly, even when tomatoes are ripe.

ONIONS

TO FRY ONIONS QUICKLY place them in a saucepan with just enough water to cover them. Bring to the boil and boil in the usual way. Strain, slice and fry for three minutes. They will quickly become golden-brown, and there is no fear of burning.

ONION-SMELL (To remove from hands): A little mustard rubbed on to the hands after peeling onions will remove the odour.

REMOVING ONION SMELL FROM DISHES: Cold water is the simplest and quickest way of removing the smell of onions or fish from dishes.

TRY SOAKING ONION IN MILK before you fry them.

HOLD ONIONS UNDER WATER when peeling them and you will not weep.

TO DRY FOR FLAVOURINGS

PUT A GOOD HANDFUL OF FRESH PARSLEY into a hot oven for a few minutes on a piece of paper. Then rub until powdery. This will keep bright green in bottle and will be always handy to sprinkle over mashed potatoes, etc., just before serving.

SAVE THE GREEN PARTS of chives, shallots and leeks, wash and dry them in a cloth and place in a cool oven to dry brown. Then crush to a powder and store in air-tight jars; use this onion powder for flavouring soups, stews, or pies.

THE OUTSIDE SKINS OF ONIONS can be dried and powdered for flavouring; pickled onions can also be used for flavouring, but in order to remove the taste of vinegar, they should be heated in the oven.

ODD BITS OF CELERY can be dried in slow oven and will keep for weeks for flavouring soups, stews, etc.

HINTS ON PASTRY MAKING

(1) The cooler the conditions when making pastry, the lighter it will be. (2) The less liquid and the more fat in the short crust, the shorter it becomes. (3) Always roll as lightly as possible, using only a little flour on board and rolling pin. (4) Brush the edges of a pie dish with cold water before putting on and lightly pressing down the cover, then make a hole in the centre of this for steam to

escape. (5) Bake pastry in a quick oven until risen. Then reduce heat and bake till crisp and golden. (6) Pastry is improved if left unwrapped in paper in a cold place overnight and then baked.

BAKING POWDER INSTEAD OF FAT. In making pastry if you use an extra teaspoonful of baking powder you can decrease the amount of fat in the recipe by one-third.

CAKES

CAKES WILL KEEP FRESH LONGER if an apple is shut in the airtight tin with them.

USE GOOD DRIPPING when making a cake—but beat it up well first and add a tablespoonful of lemon juice; prepared in this way it is just as good as butter.

CAKES FOR ICING: A cake that is to be iced should have an even crown. To obtain this, push your thumb through the centre of the uncooked paste and make a small hole. The crown of the cake will then be even and suitable for icing.

A GOOD SUBSTITUTE FOR ICING can be made by warming slightly a rounded tablespoonful of butter, beating it until creamy, then adding gradually two tablespoonfuls of golden syrup. Coloured pink with a drop of cochineal it will delight the children at Christmas.

PUTTING A CAKE INTO A WARM OVEN for a few seconds makes the icing smooth and glossy.

A SIMPLE WAY TO DECORATE A CAKE is to place a paper doyley over the top of the cake, sprinkle it liberally with sugar, then carefully remove the doyley.

ESSENCES FOR FLAVOURING should be measured out with a medicine-dropper. Pouring carelessly may ruin your cake or pudding and waste essence.

JAM SANDWICHES will be found to rise more evenly if the mixture is out in a cake tin which has been thoroughly greased, instead of employing a flat tin as is usually done.

TO PREVENT JUICE FROM BOILING OUT: When you make a fruit-pie, sprinkle a teaspoonful of cornflour on top of the fruit before covering it with pastry; this prevents the juice from boiling out.

FLAN OR OPEN TART CASE: Have you ever baked a flan case upside-down? If you haven't, try my dodge. Put the pastry over the bottom of the flan tin so that it becomes an overcoat and not a lining, and cook it like that. Don't forget to grease the tin! When it is cooked, slide the pastry off the bottom of the tin and place it the right way up.

PUDDINGS

WHEN MAKING ROLY-POLY PUDDING put into a straight-sided, greased, stone jam jar, instead of the usual pudding cloth and the shape will be much better.

TO PREVENT JAM BOILING OUT OF SUET PUDDING: Spread a thin layer of breadcrumbs over the pastry before spreading the jam.

GRATE A MEDIUM-SIZED POTATO to each pound of flour when making meat pudding; it is a splendid saving of suet.

YOUR YORKSHIRE PUDDING MUCH LIGHTER: Just a dash of water mixed with your batter before putting into oven will make your Yorkshire pudding much lighter.

WATER IN WHICH SUET PUDDINGS HAVE BEEN BOILED: stand it aside to cool and you will be surprised at the amount of fat that sets on top; this can be taken off and used for frying etc.

JELLY

TO TURN OUT WHOLE: When making jelly, lightly brush round the mould with salad oil and it will turn out whole.

JELLY IS IMPROVED if, in place of water, it is made with juice left over from either dried or fresh fruit.

TO SET JELLY QUICKLY: Stand the mould in a basin. Fill the basin with cold water to reach nearly to the top of the mould, and put a handful of kitchen salt into the water.

SUET

SUET IS A GOOD MEDIUM FOR GREASING CAKE TINS, it is not so liable to burn and makes cakes come out easily.

WHEN CHOPPING SUET: Try sprinkling the knife with a little ground rice and you will have no trouble.

FRUIT

POUR HOT WATER OVER APPLES before peeling and they can be peeled without waste.

WHEN STEWING APPLES, less sugar will be needed and the flavour much improved if the parings are boiled first and the juice used for stewing the apples instead of the usual plain water.

RHUBARB WON'T REQUIRE SO MUCH SUGAR if kept uncooked for a few days after being pulled.

TO ECONOMISE WITH SUGAR, add a pinch of soda to any stewed fruit and considerably less sugar will be required for sweetening.

LEMONS (To keep fresh): Place the lemons in a jar of cold water. Change water every day.

TO GET DOUBLE JUICE OUT OF LEMONS: Stand in boiling water before squeezing.

BLACK CURRANT LEAF flavours sweets, creams and puddings; boil in milk.

DRIED FRUIT

STORING RAISINS: When raisins are stoned a good deal of the central flesh is wasted if the ordinary plan is followed. Here is a simpler and better method: Drop the raisins in boiling water; after two or three minutes take them out one by one and squeeze them. If done properly, the stones will burst out at the stem end and no tedious cutting is needed.

DATES AND FIGS FOR PUDDINGS go farther when sprinkled with flour before chopping. This prevents the fruit caking into lumps.

DRIED FRUIT—MORE ECONOMINCAL if, after being washed and dried, the fruit is roughly cut up before mixing with other ingredients when making puddings and cakes. This sets free the juices and saves sugar.

NEVER THROW AWAY PRUNE STONES because the kernels make an excellent substitute for almonds (and almond essence) in puddings, cakes, jams, etc. Store the stones until the kernels are required (for, like nuts, the latter keep best in their natural "containers.")

CHOPPED, DRIED FIGS: Scones are delicious if you can roll in with the dough some finely-chopped, dried figs.

JAMS

A SAVING AND IMPROVEMENT ARE EFFECTED in jam making by adding 1 teaspoonful of glycerine and reducing the amount of sugar to ¾ lb. per pound of fruit; besides the saving of sugar there is less waste as there is less scum; the jam keeps longer and is clearer in colour.

JAM-COVERS WITH ADHESIVE TAPE instead of string are absolutely air-tight.

TO MAKE TWO POUNDS OF JAM INTO FOUR POUNDS: Make one pint of jelly, as directed, in a large bowl. Empty 2 lbs. jam on the jelly and stir well until thoroughly mixed; then put into jars. When set you will have 4 lbs. of delicious jam. Select jelly-flavour to suit jam: lemon or orange for marmalade.

TO GET BETTER VALUE FOR SUGAR you must use when you stew fruit, always add a pinch of salt, the same thing applies to jams and bottled fruits.

JAM TURNING MOULDY: If you find some of your home-made jam turning mouldy on the surface, scrape out the affected part; then turn the rest of the jam into a pan and boil up again. Store it in jars that are perfectly clean and dry. It will now be as good and fresh as when first made.

TO PREVENT MOULD FORMING: Rounds of tissue paper soaked in vinegar and put on the top of jam helps to prevent mould from forming.

TO KEEP JAM INDEFINITELY: Put a circle of white blotting paper on top of the waxed paper and then put the gummed cover over it all.

SALT IN JAM MAKING: If you add salt, use only half the sugar demanded by the recipe; for 4 lbs. of fruit use 2 lbs. of sugar instead of four and one teaspoonful of salt. Leave the fruit with the sugar and salt for 24 hours and then make the jam in the usual way. It will not, however, keep as long as jam made with full amount of sugar.

ANN HATHAWAY

ALSO AVAILABLE FROM PILLAR INTERNATIONAL PUBLISHING

The Young Dictator
By
Rhys Hughes

Last Orders at the Changamire Arms
by
Robin Walker

The Essential Stephen Leacock
by
Stephen Leacock

Rum Humour/Rum Humor
by
Thaddeus Lovecraft

The Unbearable Sheitness of Being
by
Thaddeus Lovecraft and Nick Faulder

Books available on Amazon.com
and
In all good bookshops

NOTES

Ad-hoc images copyright Shutterstock, RetroClipArt,
Felix Kogan, Sasha Ivv, Lineartestpilot, Nikiteev
Konstantin, Doris Rich, Ohmega1982, Abbie and Om Yos

Printed in Great Britain
by Amazon